THE WAY OF SIMPLE LOVE

the way of simple love

Inspiring Words from St. Thérèse of Lisieux

Fr. Gary Caster

franciscan
media
Cincinnati, Ohio

Contents

INTRODUCTION

The young religious sister whom St. Pius X described as "the greatest saint of modern times," spent nine years in a cloistered convent in northern France. The "Patroness of the Missions" never visited one, although she corresponded with priests who served as missionaries. The titles by which the world knows her gloss over the truth about her time in religious life: She was not that remarkable.

This is what prompted her superior (and biological sister) to ask that Sister Thérèse of the Child Jesus and the Holy Face write the story of both her life and her relationship with Jesus. The Carmelite convent in Lisieux, where another three of her sisters were members, would later use this manuscript as an obituary that they would send to other Carmelite convents after her premature death.

Thus, in obedience to her superior, Sister Thérèse composed her "spiritual autobiography," while dying from tuberculosis. Throughout it, she speaks candidly about her life as a child, her call to religious life, her love of family, and, of course, she speaks about the way in which she understands Christian discipleship. Less than twenty-five years after her death in 1897, her autobiography had spread throughout the world. The story of her life captivated women and men, especially French soldiers fighting in World War I. Her simple yet powerful explanation of living in relationship with God not only awakened hearts but also brought hope to thousands of Catholics.

Her "spiritual doctrine," popularly known as "The Little Way of Spiritual Childhood," liberated thousands of Catholics from a rigid legalistic and moralistic understanding of the faith. St. Thérèse helped people understand that sanctity was not for a limited few, but for all the baptized. Her childlike confidence and abandonment to Jesus led her to offer up to the Lord the simple duties and obligations of her religious life. She believed that nothing was too little to give Jesus, and nothing done out of love for him was insignificant. St. Thérèse was confident that Christ longed to lift everyone up to the height and depth and breadth of holiness.

On her deathbed, St. Thérèse promised to spend her time in heaven doing good upon the earth. The sign of her continued care would be "a shower of rose petals." As the time of her death drew near, her words possessed a marked enthusiasm at being able to continue serving the Lord. Those that are devoted to her know well that she makes good on her promise.

This "Little Flower" from Lisieux continues to captivate women and men today. St. John Paul II, St. Teresa of Calcutta, Pope Emeritus Benedict XVI, Dorothy Day, and many other well-known Catholic figures have had a deep devotion to St. Thérèse. St. John Paul II was so taken with the profundity of her thought that he her declared her a Doctor of the Church, giving her a place alongside such notable women as St. Teresa of Avila, St. Catherine of Siena, and St. Hildegard of Bingen. This is quite an accomplishment for a young woman who regarded herself as a little toy ball tossed aside and forgotten by Jesus. Each of our lives matter to Jesus.

Perhaps this is why so many lives still resonate with hers. It is easy to feel insignificant and unimportant. Yet, the clear and compelling language of her story and her letters remains the perfect antidote to such feelings.

The chapters that follow have been arranged according to important themes of the spiritual life, and the words that accompany these themes are entirely her own. While the language she uses might be new to you, the insights she offers are as eternal as the God who loves us and longs for each of us to be united with him, in the Son, through the Holy Spirit, for all eternity.

CHAPTER ONE

The Way of Confidence

"My way is one that is full of
confidence and love."

CONFIDENCE FROM THE GENTLE HAND OF JESUS

Yes, I desire them, these agonies of the heart, these pinpricks about which the lamb speaks. What does it matter to the little reed if it bends? It is not afraid of breaking, for it has been placed at the edge of the waters, and, instead of touching the ground when it bends, it encounters only a beneficent wave which strengthens it and makes it want another storm to come and pass over its frail head. Its weakness gives rise to all confidence. It cannot break since, no matter what happens to it, it wants only to see the gentle hand of its Jesus.

From a letter to Sister Agnes of Jesus
(her sister Marie) | JULY 1888

CONFIDENCE WHILE RESTING AT THE SIGHT OF THE TABERNACLE

It is impossible that a heart "which rests only at the sight of the Tabernacle" offend Jesus to the point of not being able to receive Him: what offends Him and what wounds His Heart is the lack of confidence! ...*receive Communion often,* very often...That is the *only remedy* if you want to be healed, and Jesus hasn't placed this desire in your soul for nothing.

From a letter to her sister Céline | MAY 1889

CONFIDENCE LEADS TO LOVE

Oh! How I would like to be able to make you understand what I feel! It is confidence and nothing but confidence that must lead us to Love...Does not fear lead to justice? Since we see the *way*, let us run together. Yes, I feel it, Jesus gives to us the same graces, He wills to give us His heaven gratuitously...I am sure that God would not give you the desire to be POSSESSED by Him, by His *Merciful Love* if He were not reserving that favor for you...or rather He has already given it to you, since you have given yourself to *Him,* since you desire to be consumed by *Him,* and since God never gives desires that He cannot realize.

From a letter to Sister Marie of the Sacred Heart
(one of Thérèse's novices) | SEPTEMBER 1896

CONFIDENCE IN BEING BORN FOR GLORY

I considered that I was born for glory, and when I searched out the means of attaining it, God inspired in me the sentiments I have just described. He made me understand my own glory would not be evident to the eyes of mortals, that it would consist in becoming a great saint! This desire could certainly appear daring if one were to consider how weak and imperfect I was, and how, after seven years in religious life, I am still weak and imperfect. I always feel, however, the same bold confidence of becoming a great saint because I don't count on my merits since I have none, but I trust in Him who is Virtue and Holiness. God alone, content with my weak efforts, will raise me to Himself and make me a saint, clothing me in His infinite merits.

Autobiography of a Soul | CHAPTER FOUR

CONFIDENT IN GOD'S JUSTICE AND MERCY

I know one must be very pure to appear before the God of all Holiness, but I know, too, that the Lord is infinitely just; and it is this justice which frightens so many souls that is the object of my joy and confidence. To be just is not only to exercise severity in order to punish the guilty; it is also to recognize right intentions and to reward virtue. I expect as much from God's justice as from His mercy. It is because He is just that, "He is compassionate and filled with gentleness, slow to punish and abundant in mercy, for He knows our frailty, He remembers we are only dust. As a father has tenderness for his children, so the Lord has compassion on us!!"

From a letter to Père Adolphe Roulland
(member, Foreign Missions of Paris) | MAY 1897

The Confident Audacity of the Saints

You love St. Augustine, St. Magdalene, these souls to whom "many sins were forgiven because they loved much." I love them too, I love their repentance, and especially…their loving audacity! When I see Magdalene walking up before the many guests, washing with her tears the feet of her adored Master, whom she is touching for the first time, I feel that *her heart* has understood the abysses of love and mercy *of the Heart of Jesus*, and, sinner though she is, this Heart of love was not only disposed to pardon her but to lavish on her the blessings of His divine intimacy, to lift her to the highest summits of contemplation.

From a letter to Abbé Maurice Bellière
(member, Missionaries of Africa) | June 1897

The Filial Confidence of God's Children

I do not believe that the heart of the happy father could resist the filial confidence of his child, whose sincerity and love he knows. He realizes, however, that more than once his son will fall into the same faults, but he is prepared to pardon him always, if his son always takes him by his heart.

From a letter to Abbé Maurice Bellière
(member, Missionaries of Africa) | July 1897

Confident in Being Always with God the Father

What a sweet joy it is to think that God is *Just*, i.e., that He takes into account our weaknesses, that He is perfectly aware of our fragile nature. What should I fear then? Ah! Must not the infinitely just God, who deigns to pardon the faults of the prodigal son with so much kindness, be just also toward me who "am with Him always?"

Autobiography of a Soul | Chapter Eight

Losing Nothing of Our Confidence

I have only to cast a glance at the Gospels and immediately I breathe in the perfumes of Jesus' life, and I know on which side to run. I don't hasten to the first place but to the last; rather than advance like the Pharisee, I repeat, filled with confidence, the publican's humble prayer. Most of all I imitate the conduct of Magdalene; her astonishing or rather her loving audacity which charms the Heart of Jesus also attracts my own. Yes, I feel it; even though I had on my conscience all the sins that can be committed, I would go, my heart broken with sorrow, and throw myself into Jesus' arms, for I know how much he loves the prodigal child who returns to Him.

Autobiography of a Soul | Chapter Eleven

Confidence in Surviving Stormy Seas

When I shall have arrived at port, I will teach you how to travel, dear little brother of my soul, on the stormy sea of the world: with the surrender and the love of a child who knows his Father loves him and cannot leave him alone in the hour of danger... The way of simple love and confidence is really made for you.

Autobiography of a Soul | Epilogue

CONFIDENCE IN GOD'S UNSPEAKABLE CONDESCENSION

O Jesus! Why can't I tell all little souls how unspeakable is Your condescension? I feel that if You found a soul weaker and littler than mine, which is impossible, You would be pleased to grant it still greater favors, provided it abandoned itself with total confidence to Your Infinite Mercy. But why do I desire to communicate Your secrets of Love, O Jesus, for was it not You alone who taught them to me, and can You not reveal them to others? Yes, I know it and I beg You to do it. I beg You to cast Your Divine Glance upon a great number of little souls. I beg You to choose a legion of *little* Victims worthy of Your LOVE!

Autobiography of a Soul | CHAPTER NINE

CONFIDENCE IN JESUS, OUR TENDER FRIEND

This, Brother, is what I think of God's justice; my way is all confidence and love. I do not understand souls who fear a Friend so tender. At times, when I am reading certain spiritual treatises in which perfection is shown through a thousand obstacles, surrounded by a crowd of illusions, my poor little mind quickly tires; I close the learned book that is breaking my head and drying up my heart, and I take up Holy Scripture. Then all seems luminous to me; a single word uncovers for my soul infinite horizons, perfection seems simple to me, I see it is sufficient to recognize one's nothingness and to abandon oneself as a child into God's arms. Leaving to great souls, to great minds the beautiful books I cannot understand, much less put into practice, I rejoice at being little since children alone and those who resemble them will be admitted to the heavenly banquet.

From a letter to Père Adolphe Roulland
(member, Foreign Missions of Paris) | MAY 1897

CHAPTER TWO

The Way of Holiness

"I don't want to be a *saint by halves.*"

HOLINESS IS CHOOSING WHAT GOD WILLS

[A]s in the days of my childhood, I cried out: "My God '*I choose all!*' I don't want to be a *saint by halves*, I'm not afraid to suffer for You, I fear only one thing: to keep my *own will;* so take it, for 'I *choose all*' that You will!"

Autobiography of a Soul | CHAPTER ONE

JESUS SETS NO LIMITS ON OUR SANCTITY

What [you] do not know perhaps is the love that Jesus has for [you], a love that demands ALL. There is nothing that is impossible for Him. He does not want to set any limit to His Lily's SANCTITY; His limit is that there is no limit! Why should there be any? We are greater than the whole universe, and one day we *ourselves* shall have a divine existence.

From a letter to her sister Céline | MARCH 1889

THE ADVANCEMENT OF ETERNITY

Life is passing away...Eternity is advancing in great strides...
Soon we shall live the very life of Jesus...After having drunk at
the fountain of all sorrows, we shall be deified at the very fountain of all joys, all delights...Soon, little sister, with one look, we
shall be able to understand what is taking place within the inner
depths of our being!

From a letter to her sister Céline | MARCH 1889

A CONQUERING SANCTITY

Sanctity does not consist in saying beautiful things, it does not
even consist in thinking them, in feeling them! It consists in
suffering and suffering *everything*. (Sanctity! We must conquer
it at the point of the sword; we must *suffer*...we *must agonize*!)

From a letter to her sister Céline | APRIL 1889

SANCTITY IS AN ASPIRATION OF THE HEART

Your prose, which you call "rough and ready," reveals to me that Jesus has placed in your heart aspirations that He gives only to souls called to the highest sanctity. Since He Himself has chosen me to be your sister, I trust He will not look upon my weakness or rather that He will use this weakness even to carry out His work, for the strong God loves to show His power by making use of nothing. United in Him, our souls will be able to save many others, for this gentle Jesus has said: "If two among you agree together on something which you ask from my Father, it will be granted them." Ah! What we are asking Him is to work for His glory, to love Him and make Him loved…How would our union and our prayer not be blessed?

From a letter to Abbé Maurice Bellière
(member, Missionaries of Africa) | FEBRUARY 1897

THE INSPIRATION FOR SANCTITY

This desire [to become a great saint] could certainly appear daring if one were to consider how weak and imperfect I was, and how, after seven years in the religious life, I still am weak and imperfect. I always feel however, the same bold confidence of becoming a great saint because I don't count on my merits since I have *none*, but I trust in Him who is Virtue and Holiness. God alone, content with my weak efforts, will raise me to Himself and make me a *saint* clothing me in His infinite merits.

Autobiography of a Soul | CHAPTER FOUR

A TOTALLY NEW WAY TO SANCTITY

I have always wanted to be a saint. Alas! I have always noticed that when I compared myself to the saints, there is between them and me the same difference that exists between a mountain whose summit is lost in the clouds and the obscure grain of sand trampled underfoot by passers-by. Instead of becoming discouraged, I said to myself: God cannot inspire unrealizable desires. I can, then, in spite of my littleness aspire to holiness. It is impossible for me to grow up, and so I must bear with myself such as I am with all my imperfections. But I want to seek out a means of going to heaven by a little way, a way that is very straight, very short, and totally new.

Autobiography of a Soul | CHAPTER TEN

THE LUMINOUS TRAIL TO THE ETERNAL SHORE

In the evening at that moment when the sun seems to bathe itself in the immensity of the waves, leaving a luminous trail behind, I went and sat down on the huge rock with Pauline. Then I recalled the touching story of the "Golden Trail." I contemplated its luminous trail for a long time. It was to me the image of God's grace shedding its light across the path the little white-sailed vessel had to travel. And near Pauline, I made the resolution never to wander far away from the glance of Jesus in order to travel peacefully toward the eternal shore!

Autobiography of a Soul | CHAPTER TWO

REAL SANCTITY

Yes, it suffices to humble oneself, to bear with one's imperfections. That is real sanctity! Let us take each other by the hand, dear little sister, and let us run to the last place...no one will come to dispute with us over it....

From a letter to Sr. Geneviève of the Holy Face
(her sister Céline) | JUNE 1897

SANCTITY AS DESTINY

Alas, it does pain Him to give us sorrows to drink, but He knows this is the only means of preparing us to "know Him as *He knows Himself* and to become *God ourselves*." Oh! What a destiny. How great is our soul....

From a letter to her sister Céline | JULY 1888

THE HEART OF SANCTITY

To you dear child I give as wedding present the last tear I shed on this earth of exile. Carry it on your heart and remember that it is through suffering that a Sister Geneviève of Saint Teresa can reach sanctity. You will have no trouble in loving the Cross and the tears of Jesus if you think often of this saying, "He loved me and He gave Himself for me!"

From a letter to Sr. Geneviève of the Holy Face
(her sister Céline) | FEBRUARY 1896

THE BRIDE IN THE CANTICLE

[St. Cecilia] became my saint of predilection, my intimate confidante. Everything in her thrilled me, especially her *abandonment*, her limitless confidence that made her capable of virginizing souls who had never desired any other joys but those of the present life. St. Cecilia is like the bride in the Canticle; in her I see "*a choir in an armed camp.*" Her life was nothing else but a melodious song in the midst of the greatest trials, and this does not surprise me because "the Gospel *rested on her heart,*" and in her heart reposed *the Spouse of Virgins*!

Autobiography of a Soul | CHAPTER SIX

CHAPTER THREE

The Way of Humility

"I desire to be forgotten,
counted for nothing."

THE POOREST IS THE MOST NOBLE

Then shall every man have praise from God and the one who on earth wanted to be the poorest, the most forgotten out of love for Jesus, will be the first, the *noblest*, and the richest!

Autobiography of a Soul | CHAPTER SIX

REAL GLORY IN BEING HIDDEN

I understood what *real glory* was. He whose kingdom is not of this world showed me that true wisdom consists in "desiring to be unknown and counted as nothing," in "placing one's joy in the contempt of self." Ah! I desired that, like the face of Jesus, "my face be truly hidden, that no one on earth would know me."

Autobiography of a Soul | CHAPTER SEVEN

POVERTY OF SOUL IGNITES THE FIRE OF LOVE

I need have no fear of purgatory. I know that of myself I would not merit even to enter that place of expiation since only holy souls can have entrance there, but I also know that the Fire of Love is more sanctifying than is the fire of purgatory. I know that Jesus cannot desire useless sufferings for us, and that He would not inspire the longings I feel unless he wanted to grant them.

Autobiography of a Soul | CHAPTER EIGHT

HUMILITY IS THE STRENGTHENING LOVE

But, it seems to me, that Jesus can give me the grace of no longer offending Him or committing faults that DON'T OFFEND Him but serve only to humble and to make love stronger.

From a letter to Sr. Agnes of Jesus
(her sister Marie) | SEPTEMBER 1890

POVERTY OF SOUL BRINGS THE GIFT OF GOD

"Lord," St. Peter answered, "we have fished all night and *have caught nothing.*" Perhaps if he had caught some *little fish*, Jesus would not have performed the miracle, but he had *nothing*, so Jesus soon filled his net in such a way as almost to break it. This is the *character* of Jesus: He gives us God, but He wills *humility of heart.*

From a letter to her sister Céline | APRIL 1894

ACKNOWLEDGING GOD'S GIFTS

Do not think that it is humility that prevents me from acknowledging the gifts of God. I know He has done great things in me, and I sing of this each day with joy. I remember that the one must love more who has been forgiven more, so I take care to make my life an act of love, and I am no longer disturbed at being a *little soul*; on the contrary, I take delight in this.

From a letter to Abbé Maurice Bellière
(member, Missionaries of Africa) | APRIL 1897

HUMILITY IS THE ANTIDOTE TO SELF-LOVE

Alas! My ardor for penances would not have lasted long had the Superiors allowed them. The penances they did allow me consisted in mortifying my self-love, which did me more good than corporeal penances.

Autobiography of a Soul | CHAPTER EIGHT

THE GREAT WORK OF THE ALMIGHTY

I am *too little* to compose beautiful sentences in order to have you believe that I have a lot of humility. I prefer to agree very simply that the Almighty has done great things in the soul of His divine Mother's child, and the greatest thing is to have shown her her *littleness*, her impotence.

Autobiography of a Soul | CHAPTER TEN

THE DESIRES OF WEAK SOULS

My desires for martyrdom *are nothing*; they are not what give me the unlimited confidence that I feel in my heart. They are, to tell the truth, the spiritual riches that *render one unjust*, when one rests in them with complacence and when one believes they *are something great*…These desires are a *consolation* that Jesus gives at times to weak souls like mine (and these souls are numerous), but when He does not give this *consolation*, it is a grace of *privilege*.

From a letter to Sr. Marie of the Sacred Heart
(one of St. Thérèse's novices) | SEPTEMBER 1896

POVERTY OF SPIRIT PLEASES JESUS

Jesus is pleased with little Céline to whom He first gave Himself for the first time thirteen years ago. He is more proud of what He is doing in her soul, of her littleness and her poverty, than He is proud of having created millions of suns and the expanse of the heavens.

From a letter to Sr. Geneviève of the Holy Face
(her sister Céline) | MAY 1897

THE POOR IN SPIRIT RECEIVE THAT WHICH IS NECESSARY

We really have to ask for indispensable things, but when we do it with humility, we are not failing in the commandment of Jesus; on the contrary, we are acting like the poor who extend their hand to receive what is necessary for them; if they are rebuked they are not surprised, as no one owes them anything.

Autobiography of a Soul | CHAPTER TEN

SERVING JESUS IN POVERTY OF SPIRIT

Ah! Let us profit from the *short moment* of life...*together* let us please Jesus, let us save souls for Him by our sacrifices... Above all, let us be *little*, so little that everybody may *trample* us underfoot, without our even having the appearance of feeling it and suffering from it.

From a letter to Sister Marie of the Trinity
(her cousin Marie Guérin) | JUNE 1897

Pushing aside Discouragement

My dear Mother, you can see that I am a *very little soul* and that I can offer God only *very little things*. It often happens that I allow these little sacrifices which give such peace to the soul to slip by; this does not discourage me, for I put up with having a little less peace and I try to be more vigilant on another occasion.

Autobiography of a Soul | Chapter Eleven

Satisfaction in Accepting Little Humiliations

One day when I particularly desired to be humiliated, a novice took it upon herself to satisfy me and she did it so well that I was immediately reminded of Shimei cursing David. I said to myself: Yes, it is the Lord who has commanded her to say all these things to me. And my soul enjoyed the bitter food served up to it in such abundance.

Autobiography of a Soul | Chapter Eleven

POVERTY OF SPIRIT LEADS TO TOTAL SURRENDER

The words of Job: "Even though he should kill me, yet will I trust him," always fascinated me in my childhood days. It took me a long time, however, to reach that degree of surrender. Now I have reached it; God has placed me in this degree, for He has taken me up into His arms and placed me there.

Autobiography of a Soul | EPILOGUE

CHAPTER FOUR

The Way of Abandonment

"On the boat itself, this one
word: Abandonment!"

ABANDONMENT: THE ONLY COMPASS

Neither do I desire any longer suffering or death, and still I love them both; it is *love* alone that attracts me, however, I desired them for a long time; I possessed suffering and believed I had touched the shores of heaven, that the little flower would be gathered in the springtime of her life. Now, abandonment alone guides me. I have no other compass! I can no longer ask for anything with fervor except the accomplishment of God's will in my soul with any creature being able to set obstacles in the way.

Autobiography of a Soul | CHAPTER EIGHT

IT IS JESUS DOING EVERYTHING IN US

In fact, directors have others advance in perfection by having them perform a great number of acts of virtue, and they are right; but my director, who is Jesus, teaches me not to count up my acts. He teaches me to do *all* through love, to refuse Him nothing, to be content when He gives me a chance of proving to Him that I love Him. But this is done in peace, in *abandonment*, it is Jesus who is doing all in me, and I am doing nothing.

From a letter to her sister Céline | JULY 1893

ABANDONMENT: THE SONG OF THE HEART

I cannot think without delight of the dear little *St. Cecilia*; what a model for the little lyre of Jesus…In the midst of the world, plunged into the center of all dangers, at the moment of being united with a young pagan who longs only for profane love, it seems to me that Cecilia would have had to tremble and to weep…but, no, while hearing the sounds of the instruments that were celebrating her nuptials, *Cecilia was singing in her heart*… What abandonment!…she *was hearing* no doubt other melodies besides those of earth, her divine Spouse *was singing* too, the angels were making resound in Cecilia's heart the sound of celestial concerts.

From a letter to her sister Céline | OCTOBER 1893

ABANDONMENT: THE ROAD TO THE DIVINE FURNACE

Jesus deigned to show me the road that leads to the Divine Furnace, and this road is the *surrender* of the little child who sleeps without fear in its Father's arms. "Whoever is a *little one* let him come to me." So speaks the Holy Spirit through the mouth of Solomon.

Autobiography of a Soul | CHAPTER NINE

SEEKING ONLY THE WILL OF JESUS

[How] different are the ways through which the Lord leads souls! In the life of the saints, we find many of them who didn't want to leave anything of themselves behind after their death, not the smallest souvenir, nor the least bit of writing. On the contrary, there are others, like our holy Mother St. Teresa, who have enriched the Church with their lofty revelations, having no fears of revealing the secrets of the King in order that they may make Him more loved and known by souls. Which of these two types of saints is more pleasing to God? It seems to me, Mother, they are equally pleasing to Him, since all of them followed the inspiration of the Holy Spirit and since the Lord has said, "*Tell the just man ALL is well.*" Yes, all is well when one seeks only the will of Jesus.

Autobiography of a Soul | CHAPTER TEN

Abandonment Is the Love to Be Unknown

"Do you want to learn something that will help you: Love to be unknown and counted as nothing!" When thinking this over I felt great peace in my soul, I felt that here was *truth* and *peace*! I was no longer disturbed about the date of my Profession, thinking that on the day when my wedding *dress* was finished, Jesus would come seeking His poor little spouse...Dear little Sister, I was not mistaken and even Jesus was content with my desire, my total abandonment.

From a letter to Sr. Françoise Thérèse-Dosithee, VHM
(her sister Léonie) | April 1895

Knowing That One Is Loved Leads to Abandonment

[We]must go to heaven by the same way, that of suffering united to love. When I shall be in port, I shall teach you, dear little Brother of my soul, how you must sail the stormy sea of the world with the abandonment and the love of a child who knows his Father loves him and would be unable to leave him in the hour of danger. Ah! How I would like to make you understand the tenderness of the Heart of Jesus, what He expects from you.

From a letter to Abbé Maurice Bellière
(member, Missionaries of Africa) | July 1897

THE EXTRAORDINARY IN THE ORDINARY

I understand and I know from experience that: *"The kingdom of God is within you."* Jesus has no need of books or teachers to instruct souls; He teaches without the noise of words. Never have I heard Him speak, but I feel the He is within me at each moment; He is guiding and inspiring me with what I must say and do. I find just what I need then, certain lights that I had not seen until then, and it isn't most frequently during my hours of prayer that these are most abundant but rather in the midst of my daily occupations.

Autobiography of a Soul | CHAPTER EIGHT

LOOKING ONLY AT JESUS

When Jesus has looked upon a soul, He immediately gives it His divine resemblance, but it is necessary that this soul not cease to fix its eyes upon Him *alone*.

From a letter to her sister Céline | APRIL 1892

THE BEAUTY OF THE SOUL IS FOUND IN ABANDONMENT

Céline! I am sure you will understand all my canticle would like to tell you, alas, I would need a tongue other than that of this earth to express the beauty of a soul's abandonment into the hands of Jesus. My heart was able only to babble what it feels... Céline, *the story of Cecilia* (the *Saint* of ABANDOMENT) is your story too! Jesus has placed near you an angel from heaven who is always looking after you.

From a letter to her sister Céline | APRIL 1894

ABANDOMENT MEANS ALLOWING GOD TO HAVE ALL

But I felt something else, that frequently God wants only *our will*; He asks *all*, and if we were to refuse Him the least thing, He loves us too much to give in to us; however, as soon as our will is conformed to His, as soon as He sees we seek Him alone, then He conducts Himself with us as in the past He conducted Himself with Abraham.

From a letter to her sister Céline | JULY 1894

CHAPTER FIVE

The Way of Obedience

"Since then Jesus made me
feel that in obeying simply, I
would be pleasing Him."

OBEDIENCE OVER SCRUPULOSITY

And so, in reality, I had only Marie, and she was indispensable to me, so to speak. I told my scruples only to her and was so obedient that my confessor never knew my ugly malady. I told him just the number of sins Marie permitted me to confess, not one more, and could pass as being the least scrupulous soul on earth in spite of the fact that I was scrupulous to the highest degree.

Autobiography of a Soul | CHAPTER FOUR

RESTING IN THE HANDS OF OBEDIENCE

I'd have liked to write to my dear Léonie, but that is impossible for me because of a lack of time. Tell her how much I am praying for her, and how much I am thinking of my dear godmother. I wanted, too, to write to little Marie, but I can't. I am praying very much so that the Blessed Virgin may make her a *little lily* that thinks very much of Jesus and *forgets itself* as well as all its miseries within the hands of obedience!

From a letter to her sister Céline | MAY 1880

THE SWEET TASK OF OBEDIENCE

I feel very unworthy to be associated in a special way with one of the missionaries of our adorable Jesus, but since obedience entrusts me with this sweet task, I am assured my heavenly Spouse will make up for my feeble merits (upon which I in no way rely), and that He will listen to the desires of my soul by rendering fruitful your apostolate.

From a letter to Père Adolphe Roulland
(member, Foreign Missions of Paris) | JUNE 1896

ONLY IF GOD WILLS IT

"Most Holy Father," answered the Vicar General, "this is *a child* who wants to enter Carmel at the age of fifteen, but the Superiors are considering the matter at the moment." "Well, my child," the Holy Father replied, looking at me kindly, "do what the Superiors tell you!" Resting my hands on his knees, I made a final effort, saying in a suppliant voice: "Oh! Holy Father, if you say yes, everybody will agree!" He gazed at me steadily, speaking these words and stressing each syllable: "Go...go... *You will enter if God wills it*!" (His accent had something about it so penetrating and so convincing, it seems to me I still hear it.)

Autobiography of a Soul | CHAPTER SIX

OBEDIENCE SHOULD ALWAYS BE ENOUGH

Well, Mother, I am obeying you and if at present, you find no interest in reading these pages, perhaps they will distract you in the future and serve to rekindle your fire, and so I will not have lost my time. But I am only joking by speaking like a child; do not believe, Mother, I am trying to discover what use my poor work can have; since I am doing it under obedience, it is enough for me, and if you were to burn it before my eyes without having read it, it would cause me no pain.

Autobiography of a Soul | CHAPTER ELEVEN

OBEDIENCE IS FREEDOM

O Mother, what anxieties the Vow of Obedience frees us from! How happy are simple religious. Their only compass being their Superiors' will, they are always sure of being on the right road; they have nothing to fear from being mistaken even when it seems that their Superiors are wrong. But when they cease to look upon the infallible compass, when they stray from the way it indicates under the pretext of doing God's will, unclear at times even to His representatives, then they wander into arid paths where the water of grace is soon lacking.

Autobiography of a Soul | CHAPTER TEN

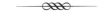

ALL IS WELL WITH OBEDIENCE

Yes, all is well when one seeks only the will of Jesus, and it is because of this that I, a poor little flower, obey Jesus when trying to please my beloved Mother…Ah! don't think Mother, that your child wants to leave you; don't think she feels it is a greater grace to die at the dawn of the day rather than at its close. What she esteems and what she desires only is to please Jesus.

Autobiography of a Soul | CHAPTER TEN

TO DRY THE TEARS OF JESUS

My only desire is to do the will of Jesus always! To dry away the little tears that sinners make Him shed…Oh! I do not want Jesus to have any sorrow. On the day of my espousal, I would like to convert *all* the sinners of this earth and to save all the souls in purgatory!

From a letter to Sr. Agnes of Jesus
(her sister Pauline) | JANUARY 1889

To Please Only Jesus

"You know where I want to go, You know for whom I want
to reach the goal. You know the one whom I love and the one
whom I want to please solely; it is for Him alone that I am
undertaking this journey. Lead me, then, by the paths which He
loves to travel. I shall be at the height of my joy provided that
He is pleased. Then Jesus took me by the hand, and He made
me enter a subterranean passage where it is neither cold nor hot,
where the sun does not shine, and in which the rain or the wind
does not visit, a subterranean passage where I see nothing but
a half-veiled light, the light which was diffused by the lowered
eyes of my Fiancé's Face…

From a letter to Sr. Agnes of Jesus
(her sister Pauline) | AUGUST 1890

OBEDIENCE MEANS LETTING JESUS GO ABOUT HIS WORK

[How] easy it is to please Jesus, to delight His Heart, one has only to love Him, without looking at one's self, without examining one's faults too much. Your Thérèse is not in the heights at this moment, but Jesus is teaching her to learn "to draw profit from everything, *from the good* and *the bad* she finds in herself." He is teaching her to play at the bank of love, or rather, He plays for her and does not tell her how He goes about it, for that is His affair, and not Thérèse's. What she must do is abandon herself, surrender herself, without keeping anything, not even the joy of knowing how much the bank is returning to her.

From a letter to Céline | JULY 1893

CHAPTER SIX

The Way of Love of God

"Not knowing how to tell
Jesus that I loved Him."

HOW SWEET TO MAKE JESUS LOVED

It seems to me that love can make up for a long life…Jesus does not look at time since there is no longer time in heaven. He must look only at love. Ask Him to give me very much love too. I'm not asking for perceptible love, but a love felt only by Jesus. Oh! To love Him and make Him loved, how sweet this is!...Tell Him, too, to take me on the day of my Profession if I must still offend Him afterward, for I'd like to carry to heaven the white robe of my second Baptism without any stain of sin on it.

From a letter to Sr. Agnes of Jesus
(her sister Pauline) | SEPTEMBER 1890

HEAVEN IS NOTHING OTHER THAN LOVE

One evening, not knowing how to tell Jesus that I loved Him and how much I desired that He be loved and glorified everywhere, I was thinking He would never receive a single act of love from hell; then I said to God that to please Him I would consent to see myself plunged into hell so that He would be *loved* in that place of blasphemy. I realized this could not give Him glory since He desires only our happiness, but when we love, we experience the need of saying a thousand foolish things; if I talked in this way, it wasn't because heaven did not excite my desire, but because at this time my heaven was none other than Love, and I felt, as did St. Paul, that nothing could separate us from the Divine Being who so ravished me!

Autobiography of a Soul | CHAPTER FIVE

PERFECT JOY IS LOVING GOD

How good He is to me, He who will soon be my Fiancé; how divinely lovable He is when not wanting to allow me to attach myself to ANY created thing. He knows well that if He were to give me a *shadow* of happiness, I would attach myself to it with all my energy, all the strength of my heart, and this shadow He is refusing me; He prefers leaving me in darkness to giving me a false light which would not be *Himself!*...Since I can't find *any* creature that contents me, I want to give all to Jesus, and I don't want to give to the creature even one *atom* of my love. My Jesus always makes me understand that He alone is perfect joy...

From a letter to Sr. Agnes of Jesus
(her sister Pauline) | JANUARY 1889

THE FLAME OF LOVE

You would like your heart to be a flame that rises up to Him without the lightest smoke. Don't forget that the smoke that surrounds you is only for yourself in order to remove from you the sight of your love for Jesus, while the flame is only for Him. At least, then He has this love entirely, for if He were to show it to us just a little bit, swiftly self-love would come like a fatal wind which extinguishes everything!

From a letter to her sister Céline | JANUARY 1889

CONSUMED BY THE LOVE OF JESUS

Why are we of this number?... A question filled with mystery... What reason can Jesus give us? Alas! His reason is that He has no reason!... Céline! Let us make use of Jesus' preference which has taught us so many things in so few years, and let us neglect nothing that can please Him!... Ah!...let us be adorned by the Sun of His *love*!...this sun is burning...let us be consumed by *love*!

From a letter to her sister Céline | APRIL 1889

A CONTINUAL SACRIFICE OF LOVE

Let us make our life a continual sacrifice, a martyrdom of love, in order to console Jesus. He wants only a *look*, a *sigh*, but a look and a sigh that are for Him *alone*!... Let all the moments of our life be for *Him alone*; let creatures touch us only in passing. There is only one thing to do during the night, the one night of life which will come only once, and this is to love, to love Jesus with all the strength of our heart and to save souls for Him so that they may be *loved*...Oh, make Jesus loved!

From a letter to her sister Céline | OCTOBER 1889

LOVE SPEAKS HEART TO HEART

Pray to the Sacred Heart; you know that I myself do not see the Sacred Heart as everybody else. I think that the Heart of my Spouse is mine alone, just as mine is His alone, and I speak to Him then in the solitude of this delightful heart to heart, while waiting to contemplate Him one day face to face.

From a letter to her sister Céline | OCTOBER 1890

LOVE CAN MAKE UP FOR A LONG LIFE

It seems to me that love can make up for a long life…Jesus does not look at time since there is no longer any time in heaven. He must look only at love. Ask Him to give me very much love too. I'm not asking for perceptible love, but a love felt only by Jesus. Oh! To love Him and make Him loved, how sweet this is!

From a letter to Sr. Agnes of Jesus
(her sister Pauline) | September 1890

LOVE ENABLES EVEN THE LEAST SACRIFICE

Which of the Thérèses will be more fervent?... The one who will be more humble, more united to Jesus, more faithful in preforming all her actions through love!... Ah! let us pray for one another in order to be equally faithful...Let us wound Jesus by our eye and by a single hair, this is, by the greatest thing and by the littlest. Let us not refuse Him the least sacrifice. Everything is so big in religion...to pick up a pin out of love can convert a soul. What a mystery! Ah! it is Jesus alone who can give such value to our actions; let us love Him with all our strength...

From a letter to Sr. Françoise Thérèse-Dosithee
(her sister Léonie) | MAY 1894

LOVE MEANS LOSING ONESELF IN GOD

He who walks in the love of God seeks neither his own gain nor his reward, but only to lose all things and himself for God; and this loss he judges to be his gain. In the evening of life, they will examine you on love. Learn then to love God as He wills to be loved and forget yourself.

From a letter to Sister Marie of the Trinity
(her cousin, Marie Guérin) | MAY 1896

THE SCIENCE OF LOVE

The science of Love, oh! Yes, this would resound sweetly in the ear of my soul. I desire only this science. Having given all my riches for it, I look upon this as having given noting, just as the spouse in the sacred canticles…I understand so well that it is only love that can make us pleasing to God that this love is the only good that I ambition. Jesus is pleased to show me the only road which leads to this divine furnace, and this road is the abandonment of the little child who sleeps without fear in his Father's arms.

From a letter to Sr. Marie of the Sacred Heart
(her sister Marie) | SEPTEMBER 1896

JESUS IS THIRSTY FOR LOVE

"Offer to God sacrifices of praise and thanksgiving." See, then, all that Jesus is asking from us. He has no need of our works but only of our *love*, for this same God, who declares he has no need to tell us if He is hungry, did not hesitate *to beg* for a little water from the Samaritan woman. He was thirsty…But when He said: Give me to drink,"…it was the *love* of His poor creature that the Creator of the universe was asking for. He was thirsty for love…

From a letter to Sr. Marie of the Sacred Heart
(her sister Marie) | SEPTEMBER 1896

———∞∞∞———

TO BE A VICTIM OF LOVE

Oh, dear Sister, I beg you, understand your little girl, understand that to love Jesus, to be His *victim of love*, the weaker one is, without desires or virtues, the more suited one is for the workings of this consuming and transforming Love... The *desire* alone to be a victim suffices, but we must be content to remain always poor and without strength, and this is the difficulty, for "The truly poor in spirit, where do we find him? You must look for him from afar," said the psalmist...He does not say that you must look for him among great souls, but "from afar," that is to say in *lowliness*, in *nothingness*...Ah! let us remain then *very far* from all that sparkles, let us love our littleness, let us love to feel nothing, then we shall be poor in spirit, and Jesus will come to look for us, and *however far* we may be, He will transform us into flames of love...

From a letter to Sr. Marie of the Sacred Heart
(her sister Marie) | SEPTEMBER 1896

WE SHALL BE JOYFUL THROUGH LOVE

All I ask Jesus for myself, I ask also for you; when I offer my weak love to the Beloved, I allow myself to offer yours at the same time. Like Joshua, you are fighting on the plain, and I am your Moses, and incessantly my heart is lifted to heaven to obtain the victory. Oh, Brother, how you would have to be pitied if Jesus were not to hold up the arms of your Moses!... But with the help of the prayer you are making each day for me to the divine Prisoner of love, I hope you will never have to be pitied and that, after this life during which we shall have sown in tears, we shall be joyful, carrying our sheaves in our hands.

From a letter to Père Adolphe Roulland
(member, Missionaries of Paris) | OCTOBER 1896

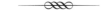

TO MAKE JESUS LOVED

You have promised to pray for me *throughout your life*; no doubt, your life will be longer than mine, and it is not permitted to forget your promise. If the Lord takes me soon with Him, I ask you to continue each day the same prayer, for I shall desire in heaven the same thing as I do on earth: To love Jesus and to make him loved.

From a letter to Abbé Maurice Bellière
(member, Missionaries of Africa) | FEBRUARY 1897

THE LORD WILL WORK MARVELS

Little Mother, why, then, is Good Jesus so *gentle* towards me? Why does he never scold me?... Ah! truly, it is enough to make me die of gratitude and love!... I am happier for having been imperfect than if, sustained by grace, I had been a model of meekness... This does me much good to see Jesus is always so gentle, so tender to me!... Ah! from this moment, I know it: yes, all my hopes will be realized... yes, the Lord will do for us marvels that will infinitely surpass our *immense desires*!

From a letter to Mother Agnes of Jesus
(her sister Pauline) | MAY 1897

THE LOVE OF THE HEART OF JESUS CASTS OUT FEAR

Ah! dear little Brother, ever since I have been given the grace to understand also the love of the Heart of Jesus, I admit that it has expelled all fear from my heart. The remembrance of my faults humbles me, draws me never to depend on my strength which is only weakness, but this remembrance speaks to me of mercy and love even more. When we cast our faults with entire filial confidence into the devouring fire of love, how would these not be consumed beyond return?

From a letter to Abbé Maurice Bellière
(member, Missionaries of Africa) | JUNE 1897

SURRENDER AND GRATITUDE: FRUITS OF LOVE

After having listened to words such as these, dear godmother, there is nothing to do but to be silent and to weep with gratitude and love. Ah! if all weak and imperfect souls felt what the least of souls feels, that is, the soul of your Little Thérèse, not one would despair of reaching the summit of the mount of love. Jesus does not demand great actions from us but simply *surrender* and *gratitude*.

Autobiography of a Soul | CHAPTER NINE

THE LAW OF LOVE

I am only a child, powerless and weak, and yet it is my weakness that gives me the boldness of offering myself as *VICTIM of Your Love, O Jesus*. In times past, victims, pure and spotless, were the only ones accepted by the Strong and Powerful God. To satisfy Divine *Justice*, perfect victims were necessary, but the *law of Love* has succeeded to the law of fear, and *Love* has chosen me as a holocaust, me, a weak and imperfect creature. Is not this choice worthy of *Love*? Yes, in order that Love be fully satisfied, it is necessary that it lower Itself, and that It lower Itself to nothingness and transform this nothingness into *fire*.

Autobiography of a Soul | CHAPTER NINE

CHAPTER SEVEN

The Way of Charity

"The mysterious depths of
charity."

LOVE IS JESUS'S OWN COMMANDMENT

When the Lord commanded His people to love their neighbor as themselves, He had not as yet come upon the earth. Knowing the extent to which each one loved himself, He was not able to ask of His creatures a greater love than this for one's neighbor. But when Jesus gave His Apostles a new commandment, HIS OWN COMMANDMENT, as He calls it later on, it is no longer a question of loving one's neighbor as oneself but of loving him as *He, Jesus, has loved him*, and will love him to the consummation of the ages.

Autobiography of a Soul | CHAPTER TEN

LOVE STRENGTHENS THE SOUL

How happy I am now for having deprived myself from the very beginning of my religious life! I already enjoy the reward promised to those who fight courageously. I no longer feel the necessity of refusing all human consolations, for my soul is strengthened by Him whom I wanted to love uniquely. I can see with joy that in loving Him the heart expands and can give to those who are dear to it incomparably more tenderness than if it had concentrated on one egotistical and unfruitful love.

Autobiography of a Soul | CHAPTER ELEVEN

LOVE IS EXPRESSED IN PRACTICING LITTLE VIRTUES

I applied myself to practicing little virtues, not having the capability of practicing the great. For instance, I loved to fold up the mantles forgotten by the Sisters, and to render them all sorts of little services. Love for mortification was given me, and this love was all the greater because I was allowed nothing by way of satisfying it.

Autobiography of a Soul | CHAPTER EIGHT

LOVE EXPRESSED IN PRAYERS FOR OTHERS

Your Benjamin comes in her turn to wish you a Happy New Year!... Just as each day has its last hour, so each year sees its last night coming also, and it is on the night of this year that I feel drawn to cast a look over the past and on the future. When I consider the time that has just run out, I feel drawn to thank God for, although His hand has offered us a bitter chalice, His divine Heart has been able to sustain us in the trial, and He has given us the strength necessary for drinking His chalice even to the last dregs. What is He reserving for us for the year that is about to begin?... I have not been given the power to penetrate this mystery, but I am begging God to reward my dear relatives a hundredfold for all the touching kindness they have for us!...

From a letter to her uncle and aunt,
the Guérins | December 1889

THE TREASURES OF GOD'S LOVE

How many memories for me there are in this date of November 19. For a long time in advance, I used to take delight in it, first, because this date was dear Aunt's feast day, and also because of the nice treats I was given on this day. Now time has passed by, the little birds have grown, they have spread their wings and have flown from the very sweet nest of childhood. But, dear little Aunt, while I was growing up, your little daughter's heart was growing also in tenderness for you, and now it understands all it owes you... To pay my debt I have only one means. Being very poor and having as my spouse a powerful and rich King, I entrust Him with pouring out in profusion on dear Aunt the treasures of His love and thus making return to her for all the motherly acts of kindness with which she surrounded my childhood.

From a letter to her aunt Madame Guérin | NOVEMBER 1890

CHARITY WINS THE HEART OF JESUS

It is my turn to make excuses, for I am very late in thanking you for all your treats, but I had faint hope of expressing my gratitude *viva voce* and I put off writing you for this reason. Oh, no! I did not have the nasty thought that my little sister was forgetting me, but I found it very natural that she was content to offer a prayer for her little Thérèse, and I was more touched than I could tell you when receiving your amiable letter. The wishes from my dear cousin were also much appreciated. Finally, the jars of jam came to crown all your acts of kindness toward me!... Our dear mother St. Teresa was so grateful that she used to say, "One could win her heart with a sardine." What would she have said had she known Francis and Jeanne?

From a letter to Madame La Néele | SEPTEMBER 1890

ALWAYS TO MAKE JESUS LOVED

I would like to save souls and forget myself for them; I would like to save them even after my death. So I would be happy if you were to say then instead of the little prayer you are saying and which will be always realized: "My God, allow my sister to make you still loved." If Jesus answers you, I shall be able to show you my gratitude."

From a letter to Père Adolphe Roulland
(member Foreign Missions of Paris) | MARCH 1897

PRAYER IS A GREAT ACT OF CHARITY

You are praying, Brother, for my parents who are in heaven, and I often pray for yours who are still on earth. This is a very sweet obligation for me, and I promise you to be always faithful in carrying it out even if I leave this exile, and even more so perhaps since I shall know better the graces necessary for them; and when their course here below is ended, I shall come to get them in your name and introduce them to heaven. How sweet will be the family life we shall enjoy throughout eternity! While awaiting this blessed eternity that will open for us in a short time, since life is only a day, let us work together for the salvation of souls. I can do very little, or rather absolutely nothing, if I am alone; what consoles me is to think that at your side I can be useful for something.

From a letter to Père Adolphe Roulland
(member, Foreign Missions of Paris) | MAY 1897

THE NECESSARY STEPS TO JESUS

Blessed is the one who places his support in Me, for he is setting in his heart steps which will lift him up to Heaven. Notice, little lamb, that I am not saying that one must separate himself *completely* from creatures, despise their love, their kindness, but, on the contrary, one *must accept* them in order to please Me, and to use them as so many *steps,* for to separate oneself from creatures would serve only one thing: *to walk* and go astray on the paths of this earth...To lift oneself up one *must place his foot* on the *steps* of creatures and attach himself to Me only.

From a letter to Mother Marie De Gonzague
(Prioress of Carmel) | JUNE 1896

ENTERTAINING JESUS

I, little Jesus, love you even though you are without any charms, and I am asking you always to spin in order to amuse me...But strokes of the whip are necessary to make the top spin...Well! Let the Sisters render you this service and be thankful to them who will be the most assiduous in not letting you relent in your spinning. When I have been well entertained by you, I will take you up above and we shall play without any suffering...

From letter to Sr. Marie of the Trinity
(one of St. Thérèse's novices) | DECEMBER 1896

LOVE: THE ONLY MEANS OF REACHING PERFECTION

Dear little Marie, as for myself, I know of no other means of reaching perfection but (love)…Love, how well our heart is made for that!… Sometimes, I seek for another word to express love, but on this earth of exile words are powerless to express all the soul's vibrations, so we have to keep to this one word (love!)… But upon whom will our poor heart hungry for love bestow it?… Ah, who will be big enough for this…will a human person be able to understand it…and, above all, will he know how to return it? Marie, there is only one Being who can understand the profundity of this word: Love!… It is only Jesus who knows how to return infinitely more than we give Him.

From a letter to her cousin Marie Guérin | JULY 1890

IT IS THE LORD THAT BUILDS THE HOUSE

I find that Jesus is very good in allowing my poor letters to do you some good, but, I assure you, I am not making the mistake of thinking I have anything to do with it. "If the Lord does not build the house, in vain do those work who build it." All the most beautiful discourses of the greatest saints would be incapable of making one *single* act of love come from a heart that Jesus did not possess.

From a letter to Céline | AUGUST 1893

OUR LOVE FOR GOD FILLS THE EMPTY HANDS OF OTHERS

I am happy to join with my Sister Geneviève in thanking you for the precious favor you obtained for our Carmel. Not knowing how to express my gratitude, I want to show you how much I was touched by your kindness to us by means of my prayers at Our Lord's feet... A feeling of sadness is mingled with my joy when learning your health was impaired, so I am asking Jesus with my whole heart to prolong your life which is so precious for the Church the longest time possible. I know the divine Master must be eager to crown you in heaven, but I trust He will leave you still in this exile so that, the immense weight of your merits may supply for other souls who present themselves before God with empty hands.

From a letter to Brother Simeon
(Discalced Carmelite in Rome) | JANUARY 1897

THE PRACTICE OF CHARITY

I must seek out in recreation, on free days, the company of Sisters who are the least agreeable to me in order to carry out with regard to these wounded souls the office of the good Samaritan. A word, an amiable smile, often suffice to make a sad soul bloom; but it is not principally to attain this end that I wish to practice charity, for I know I would soon become discouraged: any word I shall say with the best intention will perhaps be interpreted wrongly. Also, not to waste my time, I want to be friendly with everybody (and especially with the least amiable Sisters) to give joy to Jesus and respond to the counsel He gives in the Gospel: "...but when you give a feast, invite the poor, the crippled, the lame, the blind; and blessed shall you be, because they have nothing to repay you with, and your Father who sees in secret will reward you."

Autobiography of a Soul | CHAPTER NINE

JESUS'S COMMAND TO LOVE IS NOT IMPOSSIBLE

Ah! Lord, I know that you don't command the impossible. You know better than I do my weaknesses and imperfections; You know very well that never would I be able to love my Sisters as You love them, unless *You*, O my Jesus, *loved them in me*. It is because You wanted to give me this grace that You made Your *new* commandment. Oh! How I love this new commandment since it gives me the assurance that Your Will is *to love in me* all those You command me to love!

Autobiography of a Soul | CHAPTER TEN

JESUS USES OTHERS TO MAKE US GROW

For a year and a half now, Jesus has willed to change the manner of making His little flower grow. He has no doubt found her sufficiently *watered*, for now it is the *sun* that aids her growth. Jesus wants to give her nothing but His smile and this He does through you, dear Mother. This gentle sun, far from causing the little flower to wilt, makes her progress in a marvelous manner. She preserves, in the bottom of her calyx, the precious drops of dew she had received, and these serve to remind her always how little and weak she is.

Autobiography of a Soul | CHAPTER TEN

Receiving Treasures through Ordinary Experiences

Another time, I was in the laundry doing the washing in front of a Sister who was throwing dirty water into my face every time she lifted the handkerchiefs to her bench; my first reaction was to draw back and wipe my face to show the Sister who was sprinkling me that she would do me a favor to be more careful. But I immediately thought I would be very foolish to refuse these treasures which were being given me so generously, and I took care not to show my struggle. I put forth all my efforts to desire receiving much of this dirty water, and was so successful that in the end I had really taken a liking to this kind of aspersion, and I promised myself to return another time to this nice place where one received so many treasures.

Autobiography of a Soul | Chapter Eleven

JESUS DESIRES THAT WE REIGN WITH HIM THROUGH LOVE

How did Jesus love His disciples and why did He love them? Ah! it was not their natural qualities that could have attracted Him, since there was between Him and them an infinite distance. He was knowledge, Eternal Wisdom, while they were poor igno-rant fishermen filled with earthly thoughts. And still Jesus called them his *friends*, His *brothers*. He desires to see them reign with Him in the kingdom of His Father, and to open that kingdom to them. He wills to die on the cross, for he said, "*Greater love than this no man has than to lay down his life for his friends.*"

Autobiography of a Soul | CHAPTER TEN

THE REAL EFFECTS OF BEING CAPTIVATED BY JESUS

He made me understand these words of the Canticle of Canticles: "DRAW ME, WE SHALL RUN *after you in the odor of your ointments.*" O Jesus, it is not even necessary to say: *When drawing me, draw the souls whom I love*!" This simple statement: "Draw me" suffices; I understand, Lord, that when a soul allows herself to be captivated by *the odor of your ointments*, she cannot run alone, all the souls whom she loves follow in her train; this is done without constraint, without effort, it is a natural consequence of her attraction for You.

Autobiography of a Soul | CHAPTER ELEVEN

CHAPTER EIGHT

The Way of Mercy

"I will begin to sing what I must sing eternally: '*The Mercies of the Lord*.'"

THE SANCTIFYING FIRE OF MERCIFUL LOVE

Ah! since that happy day, it seems to me that *Love* penetrates and surrounds me, that at each moment, this *Merciful Love* renews me, purifying my soul and leaving no trace of sin within it…

Autobiography of a Soul | CHAPTER EIGHT

MERCY IS THE PRIVILEGE OF JESUS

Then opening the Holy Gospels my eyes fell on these words: "And going up the mountain, he called to him men of his *own choosing*, and they came to him" (St. Mark, chap. III, v. 13). This is the mystery of my vocation, my whole life, and especially the mystery of the privileges Jesus showered on my soul. He does not call those who are worthy but those whom He *pleases* or as St. Paul says: "God will have mercy on whom he will have mercy, and he will show pity to whom he will show pity. So then there is question not of him who wills nor of him who runs, but of God showing mercy" (Ep. To the Rom., chap. IX. V. 15 and 16).

Autobiography of a Soul | CHAPTER ONE

THE CONSISTENT MERCY OF GOD

It is not, then, my life, properly so-called, that I am going to write; it is my *thoughts* on the graces God deigned to grant me. I find myself at a period in my life when I can cast a glance on the past; my soul has matured in the crucible of exterior and interior trials. And now, like a flower strengthened by the storm, I can raise my head and see the words of Psalm 22 realized in me: "The Lord is my Shepherd, I shall not want; he makes me lie down in green pastures. He leads me beside still waters; he restores my soul. Even though I walk through the valley of the shadow of death, I fear no evil; for thou art with me…" To me the Lord has always been "merciful and good, slow to anger and abounding in steadfast love" (Ps. 102 v. 8)

Autobiography of a Soul | CHAPTER ONE

PRESERVED BY GOD'S MERCY

Jesus knew I was too feeble to be exposed to temptation; perhaps I would have allowed myself to be burned entirely by the *misleading light* had I seen it shinning in my eyes. It was not for me, for I encountered only bitterness where stronger souls met joy, and they detached themselves from it through fidelity. I have no merit at all, then, in not having given myself up to the love of creatures. I was preserved from it only through God's mercy! I know that without Him, I could have fallen as low as St. Mary Magdalene.

Autobiography of a Soul | CHAPTER FOUR

JESUS PLACES HIMSELF AT OUR MERCY

Oh! What a melody for my heart is this silence of Jesus... He made Himself poor that we might be able to give Him love. He holds out His hand to us like a *beggar* so that on the radiant day of judgment when He will appear in His glory, He may have us hear those sweet words: "Come, blessed of my Father, for I was hungry and you gave me to eat; I was thirsty, and you gave me to drink; I did not know where to lodge, and you gave me a home. I was in prison, sick, and your helped me." It is Jesus Himself who spoke these words; it is He who wants our love, who *begs* for it... He places Himself, so to speak, at our mercy, He does not want to take anything unless we give it to Him, and the smallest thing is precious in His divine eyes.

From a letter to her sister Céline | AUGUST 1893

MERCY: OUR ONLY TREASURE, OUR ONLY HOPE

Dear Sister, how can you say after this that my desires are the sign of my love?... Ah! I really feel that it is not this at all that pleases God in my little soul; what pleases Him is *that He sees me loving my littleness* and my *poverty, the blind hope that I have in His mercy...*

From a letter to Sr. Marie of the Sacred Heart
(her sister Marie) | SEPTEMBER 1896

GOD'S MERCY REQUIRES THAT WE LOVE MORE

Do not think that it is humility that prevents me from acknowledging the gifts of God. I know He has done great things in me, and I sing of this each day with joy. I remember that the one must love more who has been forgiven more, so I take care to make my life an act of love, and I am no longer disturbed at being a *little* soul; on the contrary, I take delight in this. That is why I dare to hope "my exile will be short," but it is not because I am prepared. I feel that I shall never be prepared if the Lord does not see fit to transform me Himself. He can do so in one instant; after all the graces He has granted me, I still await this one from His infinite mercy.

From a letter to Abbé Maurice Bellière
(member, Missionaries of Africa) | April 1897

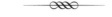

JESUS IS ALWAYS SO GENTLE

You did not scold your little girl, nevertheless, she deserved it; but your little girl is accustomed to this, your gentleness speaks more to her than severe words; you are the image of God's *mercy* for her. Yes, but…Sister St. John the Baptist, on the contrary is *usually* the image of God's *severity*. Well, I just met her, and instead of passing coldly by my side, she embraced me, saying: (absolutely as though I had been the best girl in the world) "Poor little Sister, I felt so sorry for you, I do not want to tire you out, I was wrong, etc., etc…" I, who felt contrition in my heart, was astonished at her not reproaching me in any way… When reentering our cell, I was wondering what Jesus was thinking of me, and immediately I recalled these words He addressed one day to the adulteress woman: "Has no one condemned you?" And I, tears in my eyes, answered Him, "No one Lord… Neither my little Mother or Sister St. John the Baptist, image of your justice, and really I feel I can go in peace, for You will not condemn me either!…"

From a letter to Mother Agnes of Jesus
(her sister Pauline) | MAY 1897

THE MERCY OF JESUS STRENGTHENS US

So let us line ourselves up humbly among the imperfect, let us esteem ourselves as *little souls* whom God sustains at each moment. When He sees we are very much convinced of our nothingness, He extends His hand to us. If we still wish to attempt doing something *great* even under the pretext of zeal, Good Jesus leaves us all alone. "But when I said: 'My foot has stumbled,' your mercy, Lord, strengthened me!... Ps. XCIII." Yes, it suffices to humble oneself, to bear with one's imperfections. That is real sanctity! Let us take each other by the hand, dear little sister, and let us run to the last place...no one will come to dispute with us over it...

From a letter to Sr. Geneviève of the Holy Face
(her sister Céline) | JUNE 1897

MERCY WELCOMES US INTO THE KINGDOM OF HEAVEN

When you receive this letter, no doubt I shall have left this earth. The Lord in His infinite mercy will have opened His kingdom to me, and I shall be able to draw from His treasures in order to grant them liberally to the souls who are dear to me. Believe, Brother, that your little sister will hold to her promises, and, her soul, freed from the weight of the mortal envelope, will joyfully fly toward the distant regions that you are evangelizing. Ah! Brother, I feel it, I shall be more useful to you in heaven than on earth, and it is with joy that I come to announce to you my coming entrance into that blessed city, sure that you will share my joy and thank the Lord for giving me the means of helping you more effectively in your apostolic work.

From a letter to Père Adolphe Roulland
(member, Foreign Missions of Paris) | JULY 1897

THE INFINITE MERCY OF THE LORD

I admit to you, little Brother, that we do not understand heaven in the same way. It seems to you that sharing in the justice, in the holiness of God, I would be unable as on earth to excuse your faults. Are you forgetting, then, that I shall be sharing also in the *infinite mercy* of the Lord? I believe the Blessed have great compassion on our miseries, they remember, being weak and mortal like us, they committed the same faults, sustained the same combats, and their fraternal tenderness becomes greater than it was when they were on earth, and for this reason, they never cease protecting us and praying for us.

From a letter to Abbé Maurice Bellière
(member, Missionaries of Africa) | AUGUST 1897

JESUS MERCIFULLY TENDS HIS FRUIT

When a gardener carefully tends a fruit he wants to ripen before its time, it is not to leave it hanging on a tree but to set it on his table. It was with such an intention that Jesus showered His graces so lavishly upon His little flower, He, who cried out in His mortal life: "*I thank thee, Father, that thou hast hidden these things from the wise and the prudent and revealed them to babes*," willed to have His mercy shine out in me. Because I was little and weak He lowered Himself to me, and He instructed me secretly in the *things* of His *love*. Ah! had the learned who spent their life in study come to me, undoubtedly they would have been astonished to see a child of fourteen understand perfection's secrets, secrets all their knowledge cannot reveal because to possess them one has to be poor in spirit!

Autobiography of a Soul | CHAPTER FIVE

THE LORD GRANTS THE DESIRES HE GIVES TO US

How merciful is the way God has guided me. *Never* has He given me the desire for anything which He has not given me, and even His bitter chalice seemed delightful to me.

Autobiography of a Soul | CHAPTER SEVEN

GOD'S MERCY MAKES OUR SOULS ADVANCE

Never had I heard that our faults *could not cause God any pain*, and this assurance filled me with joy, helping me to bear patiently with life's exile. I felt at the bottom of my heart that this was really so, for God is more tender than a mother, and were you not, dear Mother, always ready to pardon the little offenses I committed against you involuntarily? How often I experienced this. No word of reproach touched me as much as did one of your caresses. My nature was such that fear made me recoil; with *love* not only did I advance, I actually *flew*.

Autobiography of a Soul | CHAPTER EIGHT

MERCIFUL LOVE SETS SOULS ON FIRE

It seems to me that if You were to find souls offering themselves as victims of holocaust to Your Love, You would consume them rapidly; it seems to me, too, that You would be happy not to hold back the waves of infinite tenderness within You. If Your Justice loves to release itself, this Justice *which extends only over the earth*, how much more does Your Merciful Love desire to *set souls on fire* since Your Mercy *reaches to the heavens*. O my Jesus, let me be this happy victim; consume Your holocaust with the fire of your Divine Love!

Autobiography of a Soul | CHAPTER EIGHT

GOD'S MERCY ACCOMPANIES US FOREVER

How will this "story of a little white flower" come to an end? Perhaps the little flower will be plucked in her youthful freshness or else transplanted to other shores. I don't know, but what I am certain about is that God's Mercy will accompany her always, that it will never cease blessing the dear Mother who offered her to Jesus; she will rejoice eternally at being one of the flowers of her crown. And with this dear Mother she will sing eternally the new canticle of Love.

Autobiography of a Soul | CHAPTER EIGHT

THE FURNACE OF LOVE

As long as You desire it, O my Beloved, Your little bird will remain without strength and without wings and will always stay with its gaze fixed upon You. It wants to be *fascinated* by Your divine glance. It wants to become the *prey* of Your Love. One day I hope that You, the Adorable Eagle, will come fetch me, Your little bird; and ascending with it to the Furnace of Love, You will plunge it for all eternity into the burning Abyss of this Love to which it has offered itself as victim.

Autobiography of a Soul | CHAPTER NINE

GOD'S MERCY BRINGS UNEXPECTED CONSOLATIONS

All this, however, does not prevent both distractions and sleepiness from visiting me, but at the end of the thanksgiving when I see that I've made it so badly I make a resolution to be thankful all through the rest of the day. You see dear Mother, that I am far from being on the way of fear; I always find a way to be happy and to profit from my miseries; no doubt this does not displease Jesus since He seems to encourage me on this road. Contrary to my usual state of mind, one day I was a little disturbed when going to Communion; it seemed to me that God was not satisfied with me and I said to myself: Ah! if I receive only half a host today, this will cause me great sorrow and I shall believe that Jesus comes regretfully into my heart. I approached, and oh, what joy! For the first time in my life I saw the priest take two hosts which were well separated from each other and place them on my tongue! You can understand my joy and the sweet tears of consolation I shed when beholding a mercy so great!

Autobiography of a Soul | CHAPTER EIGHT

GOD SURPASSES ALL EXPECTATIONS

O my God, You surpassed all my expectation. I want only to sing to Your mercies. "You have taught me from my youth, O God, and until now I will declare Your wonderful works. And until old age and gray hairs, O God forsake me not." What will this old age be for me? It seems this could be right now, for two thousand years are not more in the Lord's eyes than are twenty years, than even a single day.

Autobiography of a Soul | CHAPTER TEN

LOVING JESUS TO THE POINT OF DYING OF LOVE

Never have I felt before this, dear Mother, how sweet and merciful the Lord really is, for He did not send me this trial until the moment I was capable of bearing it. A little earlier I believe it would have plunged me into a state of discouragement. Now it is taking away everything that could be a natural satisfaction in my desire for heaven. Dear Mother, it seems to me now that nothing could prevent me from flying away, for I no longer have any great desire except that of loving to the point of dying of love.

Autobiography of a Soul | CHAPTER TEN

CRUMBS THAT FALL FROM THE MASTER'S TABLE

This is the way God sees fit to take care of me. He cannot always be giving me the strengthening bread of exterior humiliation, but from time to time He allows *me to be fed the crumbs which fall from the table OF HIS CHILDREN*. Ah! how great is His mercy; I shall be able to sing of it only in heaven.

Autobiography of a Soul | CHAPTER ELEVEN

LIFTING THE WORLD THROUGH GOD'S MERCY

A scholar has said: "*Give me a lever and a fulcrum and I will lift the world.*" What Archimedes was not able to obtain, for his request was not directed by God and was only made from a material viewpoint, the saints have obtained in all its fullness. The Almighty has given them as *fulcrum: HIMSELF ALONE;* as *lever:* PRAYER which burns with a fire of love. And it is in this way that they have *lifted the world*; it is in this way that the saints militant lift it, and that, until the end of time, the saints to come will lift it.

Autobiography of a Soul | CHAPTER ELEVEN

CHAPTER NINE

The Way of Our Lady

"Father encouraged me to
be devout to the Blessed
Virgin."

THE CARE OF THE BLESSED VIRGIN

The Blessed Virgin, too, watched over her little flower and, not wanting her to be tarnished by contact with worldly things, drew her to her mountain before she blossomed.

Autobiography of a Soul | CHAPTER FOUR

THE SORROWS OF MARY AND JOSEPH

Oh! never had I understood so well as during this trial, the sorrow of Mary and Joseph during their three-day search for the divine Child Jesus. I was in a sad desert, or rather, my soul was like a fragile boat delivered up to the mercy of the waves and having no pilot. I knew Jesus was there sleeping in my boat, but the night was so black it was impossible to see Him; nothing gave me any light, not a single flash came to break the dark clouds.

Autobiography of a Soul | CHAPTER FIVE

THE INTERCESSION OF THE BLESSED VIRGIN

The Blessed Virgin, nevertheless, was helping me prepare the dress of my soul; as soon as the dress was completed all the obstacles went away by themselves. The Bishop sent me the permission I had sought, the community voted to receive me, and my Profession was fixed for September 8, 1890.

Autobiography of a Soul | CHAPTER SEVEN

SPEAKING TO THE MOTHER IN HEAVEN

In the afternoon, it was I who made the Act of Contrition to the Blessed Virgin. It was only right that I speak in the name of my companions to my Mother in heaven, I who had been deprived at such an early age of my earthly Mother. I put all my heart into speaking to her, into consecrating myself to her as a child throwing itself into the arms of its mother, asking her to watch over her. It seems to me the Blessed Virgin must have looked upon her little flower and smiled at her, for wasn't it she who cured her with a visible smile? Had she not placed in the heart of her little flower her Jesus, the Flower of the Fields and the Lily of the valley?

Autobiography of a Soul | CHAPTER FOUR

THE VIRGIN OF THE SMILE

I was suffering very much from this forced and inexplicable struggle and Marie was suffering perhaps even more than I. After some futile attempts to show me she was by my side, Marie knelt down near my bed with Léonie and Céline. Turning to the Blessed Virgin and praying with the fervor of a mother begging for the life of her child, Marie obtained what she wanted... Finding no help on earth, poor little Thérèse had also turned toward the Mother of heaven, and prayed with all her heart that she take pity on her. All of a sudden the Blessed Virgin appeared beautiful to me, so beautiful that never had I seen anything so attractive; her face as suffused with an ineffable benevolence and tenderness, but what penetrated to the very depths of my soul was the "ravishing smile of the Blessed Virgin." At that instant, all my pain disappeared, and two large tears glistened on my eyelashes, and flowed down my cheeks silently, by they were tears of unmixed joy. Ah! I thought, the Blessed Virgin smiled at me, how happy I am, but never will I tell anyone for my happiness would then disappear... Seeing my gaze fixed on the Blessed Virgin, [Marie] cried out: "Thérèse is cured!"

Autobiography of a Soul | CHAPTER THREE

HAVING TO SHARE THAT WHICH IS MOST SECRET

In their presence [the sisters of the Carmel] I was questioned about the grace I had received. They asked me if the Blessed Virgin was carrying the Child Jesus, or if there was much light, etc. All these questions troubled me and caused me much pain, and I was able to say only one thing: "The Blessed Virgin had appeared very beautiful, and I had seen her smile at me." It was her countenance alone that had struck me, and seeing that the Carmelites had imagined something else entirely (my spiritual trials beginning already with regard to sickness), I thought I had lied. Without any doubt, if I had kept my secret I would also have kept my happiness, but the Blessed Virgin permitted this torment for my soul's good, as perhaps without it I would have had some thought of vanity, whereas humiliation becoming my lot, I was unable to look upon myself without a feeling of profound horror. Ah! what I have suffered I shall not be able to say except in heaven!

Autobiography of a Soul | CHAPTER THREE

CHILD OF OUR LADY OF VICTORIES

Poor little Father tired himself out trying to please us, and very soon we saw all the marvels of the Capital. I myself found *only one* which filled me with delight, *Our Lady of Victories!* Ah! what I felt kneeling at her feet cannot be expressed. The graces she granted me so moved me that my happiness found expression only in tears, just as on the day of my First Communion. The Blessed Virgin made me feel *it was really herself who smiled on me and brought about my cure.* I understood she was watching over me, that I was *her* child.

Autobiography of a Soul | CHAPTER SIX

TO THE PURE ALL THINGS ARE PURE

I prayed to Our Lady of Victories to keep far from me everything that could tarnish my purity; I was fully aware that on a voyage such as this into Italy I could easily meet with things capable of troubling me. I was still unacquainted with evil and so was apprehensive about making its discovery. I had not yet experienced that *to the pure all things all pure,* that the simple and upright soul sees evil in nothing since it resides only in impure hearts, not in inanimate objects.

Autobiography of a Soul | CHAPTER SIX

MARY CONQUERS DEMONS

The sickness which overtook me certainly came from the demon; infuriated by your entrance into Carmel, he wanted to take revenge on me for the wrong our family was to do him in the future. But he did not know that the sweet Queen of heaven was watching over her fragile little flower, that she *was smiling* on her from her throne in heaven and was preparing to stop the storm the moment her flower was to break without any hope of recovery.

Autobiography of a Soul | CHAPTER THREE

MARY PRESENTS US TO HER SON JESUS

This beautiful day passed by just as do the saddest since the most radiant day has a tomorrow; it was without sadness, however, that I placed my crown at the Blessed Virgin's feet. I felt that time could not take away my happiness. Mary's nativity! What a beautiful feast on which to become the spouse of Jesus! It was the *little Blessed Virgin, one day old, who was presenting her* little *flower* to the *little* Jesus.

Autobiography of a Soul | CHAPTER EIGHT

THE QUEEN OF HEAVEN IS SATISFIED WITH OUR EFFORTS

(I am ashamed to admit it), the recitation of the rosary is more difficult for me than the wearing of an instrument of penance. I feel I have said this so poorly! I force myself in vain to meditate on the mysteries of the rosary; I don't succeed in fixing my mind on them. For a long time I was desolate about this lack of devotion that astonished me, for I *love* the Blessed Virgin so much that it should be easy for me to recite in her honor prayers which are so pleasing to her. Now I am less desolate; I think that the Queen of heaven, since she is *my MOTHER*, must see my good will and she is satisfied with it.

Autobiography of a Soul | CHAPTER ELEVEN

THE BLESSED VIRGIN IS OUR PROTECTION

The Blessed Virgin shows me she is not displeased with me, for she never fails to protect me as soon as I invoke her. If some disturbance overtakes me, some embarrassment, I turn very quickly to her and as the most tender of Mothers she always takes care of my interests. How many times, when speaking to the novices, has it happened that I invoked her and felt the benefits of her motherly protection!

Autobiography of a Soul | CHAPTER ELEVEN

PREPARING TO RECEIVE HOLY COMMUNION

I can't say that I frequently received consolations when making my thanksgivings after Mass; perhaps it is the time when I receive the least. However, I find this very understandable since I have offered myself to Jesus not as one desirous of her own consolation in His visit but simply to please Him who is giving Himself to me. When I am preparing for Holy Communion, I picture my soul as a piece of land and I beg the Blessed Virgin to remove from it *any rubbish* that would prevent it from being *free*; then I ask her to set up a huge tent worthy of *heaven*, adorning it with *her own* jewelry; finally I ask all the angels and saints to come and conduct a magnificent concert there.

Autobiography of a Soul | CHAPTER EIGHT

ASKING FOR OUR LADY'S ASSISTANCE

Before taking up my pen, I knelt before the statue of Mary (the one that has given me so many proofs of the maternal preferences of heaven's Queen for our family), and I begged her to guide my hand that it trace no line displeasing to her.

Autobiography of a Soul | CHAPTER ONE

CHILDREN OF MARY

I was very much touched by your kind attention. I received the dear circular letter of the Children of Mary with pleasure. Certainly, I won't fail to be present in spirit at this beautiful celebration, for was it not in this beautiful chapel that the Blessed Virgin adopted me on the beautiful day of my First Communion and on the day of my reception into the Children of Mary.

From a letter to Mother Saint-Placide, VHM
(prioress of the Visitation Convent in Caen) | DECEMBER 1888

HAVING RECOURSE TO OUR BLESSED LADY

Little sister, before I received your letter, I had a presentiment of your anxiety; my heart was united to your heart. Last night, in my dreams, I tried to console you, but, alas! I was unable to succeed!... I am not going to be any more fortunate today unless Jesus and the Blessed Virgin come to my help; I hope my desire will be fulfilled and that on the last day of her month, the Blessed Virgin will heal my dear little sister. But for this you must pray, *pray very much*. If you could only place a candle at *Notre-Dame-des-Victoires*... I have so much confidence in her...

From a letter to her cousin Marie Guérin | MAY 1889

HANDLING SOULS WITH THE TENDERNESS OF MARY

Let us not waste our time, soon eternity will shine for us!... Céline, if you wish, let us convert souls: this year , we must form many *priests* who love Jesus! And who handle Him with the same *tenderness* with which Mary *handled* Him in His cradle!

From a letter to her sister Céline | December 1889

THE GRACE OF BEING THE FAMILY OF JESUS

Ah, what a grace to be a virgin, to be a spouse of Jesus. It must be very beautiful, very sublime, since the purest, most intelligent of all other creatures preferred to remain a virgin rather than become the Mother of God...And this is the grace Jesus grants us. He wants us to be His spouses, and then He promises that we shall be His mother and His sisters, for He says in the gospel: "He who does the will of my Father, he is My Mother, my brother, and my sister," Yes, the one who loves Jesus is His whole family. He finds in this *unique* heart, which does not have its LIKE, all that He desires; He finds His heaven there!

From a letter to her sister Céline | July 1891

More Blessed Than Our Lady

With regard to the Blessed Virgin, I must confide to you one of my simple ways with her. I surprise myself at times by saying to her: "But good Blessed Virgin, I find I am more blessed than you, for I have you for Mother, and you do not have a *Blessed Virgin to love*…It is true you are the Mother of Jesus, but this Jesus you have given entirely to us…and He, on the Cross, He gave you to us as Mother. Thus we are richer than you since we possess Jesus and since you are ours also. Formerly, in your humility, you wanted one day to be the little servant of the happy Virgin who would have the honor of being the Mother of God, and here I am, a poor little creature, and I am not your servant but your child. You are the Mother of Jesus, and you are my Mother." No doubt the Blessed Virgin must laugh at my simplicity, and nevertheless what I am telling her is really true!

From a letter to her sister Céline | October 1892

Loving Our Lady

Have no fear of loving the Blessed Virgin *too much*, you will *never* love her enough, and Jesus will be pleased since the Blessed Virgin is His Mother.

From a letter to her aunt Madame Guérin | May 1889

MARY AND THE DAY OF PROFESSION

On February 24, at midnight, St. Peter will open the portals of heaven, and immediately the angels and saints will go forth with incomparable joy to form the court of the King and His fiancée. The Virgin Mary, immediately preceding the Adorable Trinity, will advance, carrying the royal adornment of the spouse, her dear daughter. With all-motherly care, she will open the abyss of purgatory before descending to earth. Instantly, innumerable multitudes of souls will fly toward their liberatrix, desiring to thank her and to learn the reason for their unexpected deliverance. The gentle Queen will answer: "Today is my Son's wedding. On the earth of exile, He has chosen from all eternity a soul that charms and delights Him, among the millions of others whom He has nonetheless created according to His image. This chosen soul offered this prayer to me: 'On the day of my wedding, I would like all suffering to be banished from my Bridegroom's kingdom.' Answering her appeal, I am coming to deliver you… take your place in our cortege, sing with the blessed the favors of Jesus and Céline."

From a letter to Sr. Geneviève of the Holy Face
(her sister Céline) | February 1896

THE GRACES MARY OBTAINS FOR MISSIONARIES

It is true that no human life is exempt from faults; only the Immaculate Virgin presents herself absolutely pure before the divine Majesty. Since she loves us and since she knows our weakness, what have we to fear? Here are a lot of sentences to express my thought, or rather not to succeed in expressing it, I wanted simply to say that it seems to me all missionaries are *martyrs* by desire and will and that, as a consequence, not one should have to go to purgatory. If there remains in their soul at the moment of appearing before God some trace of human weakness, the Blessed Virgin obtains for them the grace of making an act of perfect love, and then she gives them the grace of the crown that they so greatly merited.

From a letter to Père Adolphe Roulland
(member, Foreign Missions of Paris) | MAY 1897

THE CONSOLATIONS OF THE BLESSED VIRGIN

Ah! I beg you, pray very much for me, prayers are so necessary for me at this moment; but *above all* pray for *our Mother*. She would have liked to hold me back here below for still a long time, and to obtain it this venerable Mother has had a novena of Masses offered to *Notre-Dame des Victoires*, who had already cured me in my childhood; but I, feeling that the miracle would not take place, asked and obtained from the Blessed Virgin that she console my Mother's heart a little, or rather that she make her consent to Jesus' taking me away to heaven.

From a letter to Abbé Maurice Bellière
(member, Missionaries of Africa) | JULY 1897

DRYING THE TEARS OF JESUS

Let us raise ourselves above what is passing away. Let us keep ourselves a distance from the earth. Higher up the air is pure. Jesus is hiding Himself, but we can see Him. When shedding tears, we are drying His, and the Blessed Virgin smiles.

From a letter to her sister Céline | JULY 1888

COMMENDING TO OUR LADY'S CARE

Brother, you will not have time to send me your messages for heaven, but I am guessing at them, and then you will only have to tell me them in a whisper, and I shall hear you, and I shall carry your messages faithfully to the Lord, to our Immaculate Mother, to the Angels, and to the Saints whom you love. I will ask the palm of martyrdom for you, and I shall be near you, holding your hand so that you may gather up this glorious palm without effort, and then with joy we shall fly together into the heavenly homeland, surrounded by all the souls who will be your conquest.

From a letter to Père Adolphe Roulland
(member, Foreign Missions of Paris) | JULY 1897

WORKING FOR THE SALVATION OF SOULS

Let us work together for the salvation of souls; we have only one day of this life to save them and thus to give the Lord proofs of our love, The tomorrow of this day will be eternity, and then Jesus will restore to you a hundredfold the very sweet and very legitimate joys that you sacrificed for Him. He knows the extent of your sacrifice, He knows the suffering of those dear to you increases your own, but He also suffered this martyrdom. To save our souls He left His Mother, He saw the Immaculate Virgin standing at the foot of the Cross, her heart transpierced by a sword of sorrow. So I hope our divine Savior will console your good mother, and I am asking Him for this immediately. Ah! if the divine Master allowed those whom you are leaving for His love to glimpse the glory He is reserving for you, the multitude of souls who will make up your cortege in heaven, they would already be rewarded for the great sacrifice your separation will cause them.

From a letter to Abbé Maurice Bellière
(member, Missionaries of Africa) | December 1896

CHAPTER TEN

The Way of Suffering

"How merciful is the way
God has guided me...even
His bitter chalice seemed
delightful."

SUFFERING AND GLORY

I understood what *real glory* was. He whose Kingdom is not of this world showed me that true wisdom consists in "desiring to be unknown and counted as nothing," in "placing one's joy in contempt of self." Ah! I desired that, like the Face of Jesus, "my face be truly hidden, that no one on earth would know me." I thirsted after suffering and I longed to be forgotten.

Autobiography of a Soul | CHAPTER SEVEN

GIVING REST TO OUR LORD

I should have spoken to you about the retreat preceding my Profession, dear Mother, before speaking about the trial I have mentioned; it was far from bringing me any consolations since the most absolute aridity and almost total abandonment were my lot. Jesus was sleeping as usual in my little boat; ah! I see very well how rarely souls allow Him to sleep peacefully within them. Jesus is so fatigued with always having to take the initiative and to attend to others that He hastens to take advantage of the repose I offer to Him. He will undoubtedly awaken before my great eternal retreat, but instead of being troubled about it, this only gives me extreme pleasure.

Autobiography of a Soul | CHAPTER EIGHT

THE DREAM OF MARTYRDOM

Martyrdom was the dream of my youth and this dream has grown with me within Carmel's cloisters. But here again, I feel that my dream is folly, for I cannot confine myself to desiring *one kind* of martyrdom. To satisfy me I need *all*. Like You, my Adorable Spouse, I would be scourged and crucified. I would die flayed like St. Bartholomew. I would be plunged into boiling oil like St. Kohn; I would undergo all the tortures inflicted upon the martyrs. With St. Agnes and St. Cecilia, I would present my neck to the sword, and like Joan of Arc, my dear sister I would whisper at the stake Your Name, O Jesus.

Autobiography of a Soul | CHAPTER NINE

SUFFERING AND JOY

I really feel that I would have no disappointment, for when one expects pure and unmixed suffering, the smallest joy becomes an unhoped-for surprise. And you know, Mother, that suffering itself becomes the greatest joys when one seeks it as the most precious of treasures.

Autobiography of a Soul | CHAPTER TEN

Hidden and Forgotten

Dear Mother, as you told me, a very special vocation is necessary to live in foreign Carmels. Many believe they are called to this, but it isn't so. You told me, too, that I had this vocation and only my poor health stood in the way. I know very well this obstacle would disappear if God were calling me to the missions, and so I live without any unrest. If I have to leave my dear Carmel someday it would not be without pain, for Jesus has not given me an indifferent heart. And precisely because my heart is capable of suffering I want it to give Jesus everything possible. *Here*, dear Mother, I live without any burdens from the cares of this miserable earth, and have only to accomplish the sweet and easy mission you have confided to me. *Here*, I receive your motherly attention and do not feel the pinch of poverty since I never lack anything. But *here*, above all, I am loved by you and all the Sisters, and this affection is very sweet to me. This is why I dream of a monastery where I shall be unknown, where I would suffer from poverty, the lack of affection, and finally, the exile of the heart.

Autobiography of a Soul | Chapter Ten

ALL FOR LOVE OF JESUS

Before "*resting in the shadow of him whom I desired*," I was to pass through many trials, but the divine call was so strong that had I been forced to *pass through flames*, I would have done it out of love for Jesus.

Autobiography of a Soul | CHAPTER FIVE

THE UNSPEAKABLE SWEETNESS OF JESUS

The day after my Communion, ... I felt born within me the *great desire* to suffer, and at the same time the interior assurance that Jesus reserved a great number of crosses for me. I felt myself flooded with consolations so *great* that I look upon them as one of the *greatest* graces of my life. Suffering became my attraction; it had charms about it which ravished me without my understanding them very well. Up until this time, I had suffered without *loving* suffering, but since this day I felt a real love for it. I also felt the desire of loving only God, of finding my joy only in Him. Often during my Communions, I repeated these words of the Imitation: "O Jesus, unspeakable *sweetness*, change all the consolations of this earth into *bitterness* for me." This prayer fell from my lips without effort, without constraint; it seemed I repeated it not with my will but like a child who repeats the words a person he loves has inspired in him.

Autobiography of a Soul | CHAPTER FOUR

RELIGIOUS LIFE AND SUFFERING

I found the religious life to be *exactly* as I had imagined it, no sacrifice astonished me and yet, as you know, dear Mother, my first steps met with more thorns than roses! Yes, suffering opened wide its arms to me and I threw myself into them with love. I had declared at the feet of Jesus-Victim, in the examination preceding my Profession, what I had come to Carmel for: "I came to save souls and especially to pray for priests." When one wishes to attain a goal, one must use the means; Jesus made me understand that it was through suffering that He wanted to give me souls, and my attraction for suffering grew in proportion to its increase. This was my way for five years; exteriorly nothing revealed my suffering, which was all the more painful since I alone was aware of it. Ah! what a surprise we shall have at the end of the world when we shall read the story of souls! There will be those who will be surprised when they see the way through which my soul was guided!

Autobiography of a Soul | CHAPTER SEVEN

Spiritual Aridity and Suffering

One day, in heaven, we shall love talking to one another about our *glorious* trials; don't we already feel happy for having suffered them? Yes, Papa's three years of martyrdom appear to me as the most loveable, the most fruitful of my life; I wouldn't exchange them for all the ecstasies and revelations of the saints. My heart overflows with gratitude when I think of this inestimable *treasure* that must cause a holy jealousy to the angels of the heavenly court. My desire for suffering was answered, and yet my attraction for it did not diminish. My soul soon shared in the sufferings of my heart. Spiritual aridity was my daily bread and, deprived of all consolation, I was still the happiest creatures since all my desires had been satisfied.

Autobiography of a Soul | Chapter Seven

To Drink the Chalice of Suffering

For a long time I have not belonged to myself since I delivered myself totally to Jesus, and He is therefore free to do with me as He pleases. He has made me *understand all the sufferings* I would meet with, asking me if I would want to drink this chalice to the dregs; I wanted to seize this cup immediately when Jesus presented it, but He withdrew His hand and made me understand that my resignation alone was pleasing to Him.

Autobiography of a Soul | Chapter Ten

THE DESIRE FOR TRIALS

[The] One whom I love is not at a loss as to the means He uses. Without changing my way He sent me the trial which was to mingle a salutary bitterness with all my joys. It is not only when He wishes to try me that Jesus makes me feel and desire trials.

Autobiography of a Soul | CHAPTER ELEVEN

SUFFERING ENABLES A GREATER LOVE OF GOD

Oh, yes! Pauline, when Jesus will have set me on the blessed shore of Carmel, I want to give myself totally to Him. I want to live only for Him. Oh! No, I shall not fear His strikes, for even in the most bitter sufferings, I always feel that it is His hand that strikes (He has really shown me this). I have felt it at Rome at the moment when I would have believed that the earth would give away beneath my steps. I desire only one thing when I am in Carmel, it is always (to preserve my place) to suffer for Jesus. Life passes so quickly that truly it must be better to have a very beautiful crown and a little trouble than (not) to have an ordinary one without any trouble and then for a suffering born with joy, when I think that for all eternity I shall love God better. Then in suffering, one can save souls.

From a letter to Sr. Agnes of Jesus
(her sister Pauline) | March 1888

A Day without Suffering Is a Day Lost

Tomorrow, it will be a month that I am far from you, but it seems to me that we are not separated. What does the place matter where we are? Even if the ocean were to separate us, we would remain united, for our desires are the same and our hearts beat together...I am sure that you understand me. (What does it matter after all whether life is cheerful or sad, we would nonetheless reach the end of our journey here below). A day of a Carmelite spent without suffering is a day lost. For you it is the same thing, for you are a Carmelite at heart.

From a letter to her sister Céline | May 1888

Giving Birth to Souls

I had the happiness of contemplating for a long time the marvels *Jesus* is working by means of my dear Mother. I see that *suffering alone* gives birth to souls, and more than ever before these sublime words of Jesus unveil their depths to me: *"Amen, amen I say to you, unless the grain of wheat falls into the ground and dies, it remains alone; but if it dies, it will bring forth much fruit."*

Autobiography of a Soul | Chapter Eight

JESUS ALONE IS OUR FRIEND

If we feel Jesus present, oh! Then we would really do all for Him, but no, He seems a thousand leagues away. We are all alone with ourselves. Oh! What annoying company when Jesus is not there. But what is this sweet Friend doing then? Doesn't He see our anguish, the weight that is oppressing us? Where is He? Why doesn't He come to console us since we have Him alone for a friend? Alas, He is not far; He is there, very close. He is looking at us, and He *is begging* this sorrow, this agony from us. He needs it for souls and for our soul. He wants to give us such a beautiful recompense, and His ambitions for us are very great. But how can He say: "My turn," if ours hasn't come, if we have given Him nothing? Alas, it does pain Him to give us sorrows to drink, but He knows this is the only means of preparing us to "know Him as *He knows Himself* and to become *Gods ourselves*." Oh! What a destiny. How great is our soul…

From a letter to her sister Céline | JULY 1888

116

MAKING JESUS SMILE

When I think that if God were to give us the entire universe with all its treasures that this would not be comparable to the *lightest* suffering! What a grace when, in the morning, we feel no courage, no strength to practice virtue; that is the moment to put the axe to the root of the tree. Instead of wasting our time gathering a few baubles, we can dip into the diamonds, and what a profit at the end of the day…It is true that sometimes, for a few moments, we look with scorn at gathering our treasures, and this is the difficult moment. We are tempted to leave all behind, but in one act of love, even *unfelt* love, all is repaired, and Jesus smiles.

From a letter to her sister Céline | October 1888

THE CHOSEN FRIENDS OF JESUS

This morning, during my Holy Communion, I prayed very much to Jesus to give you His joys; alas! This is not what He is sending us for some time. It is the Cross, the Cross alone, which He is giving us in order to test us…Oh! Aunt, if it had been only myself who was suffering, this would have been nothing, but I know the large share you took in our trial. For your feast, I would like to take away all sorrow and to take for myself all your pains. This is what I was asking for just now from Him whose Heart beats in union with my own. I then felt that all He could give us of the best was suffering, and He was giving this only to His *chosen* friend; this answer proved to me that I was not answered, for I saw that Jesus loved dear Aunt too much to take away the Cross.

From a letter to her aunt Madame Guérin | NOVEMBER 1888

THE GENEROUS HEART OF SUFFERING

Ask Jesus to make me generous during my retreat. He is riddling me with *pinpricks*; the poor little ball is exhausted. All over it has very little holes which make it suffer more than if it had only one large one!... Nothing near Jesus. Aridity!... Sleep!... But at least there is silence!... Silence does good to the soul... But creatures! Oh! Creatures!... The little ball shudders from them!... Understand Jesus' little toy!...When it is the sweet Friend who punctures His ball Himself, suffering is only sweetness, His hand is *so gentle*! ...but creatures!... Those who surround me are very good, but there is something, I don't know what, that repels me!... I cannot give you any explanation. Understand your little soul. I am, however, very *happy*, happy to suffer what Jesus wants me to suffer. If He doesn't directly puncture His little ball, it is really He who directs the hand that punctures it!

From a letter to Sr. Agnes of Jesus
(her sister Pauline) | JANUARY 1888

DRINKING FROM THE SPRING OF JESUS

Why seek joy on earth; I admit to you that my heart has a burning thirst for it, but this heart sees that no creature is capable of quenching its thirst. On the contrary, the more it drinks at this delightful spring the more burning does its thirst become!...I know another spring; it is the one at which, after one has drunk, one is still thirsty, but with a thirst that is not panting. It is very sweet, on the contrary, because it has something satisfying in it, and this spring is the suffering that is known to Jesus alone.

From a letter to Sr. Marie of the Sacred Heart
(her sister Marie) | JANUARY 1889

THE PEACE OF CHRIST IS GREATER THAN CONSOLATIONS

Today more than yesterday, if that were possible, I was deprived of all consolation. I thank Jesus, who finds this good for my soul, and that, perhaps if He were to console me, I would stop at this sweetness; but He wants that *all* be for *Himself*!...Well, then, *all* will be for Him, all, even when I feel I am able to offer nothing; so, just like this evening, I will give Him this nothing! Although Jesus is giving me no consolation, He is giving me a peace so great that it is doing me more good!...

From a letter to Sr. Agnes of Jesus
(her sister Pauline) | JANUARY 1889

What Do the Things of this Earth Matter?

The things of this earth...what do they mean to us? ... Should this be our homeland, this *slime*, so unworthy of an immortal soul...and what does it matter to us that cowardly men *harvest* the mustiness that grows on this slime? The more our heart is in heaven the less we feel these *pinpricks*...But believe that this is a *grace* and a *great grace* to feel these pinpricks, for, them, our life is a *martyrdom*, and one day Jesus will give us the palm. To suffer and to be *despised*!...what *bitterness* but what glory.

From a letter to her sister Céline | January 1889

Life Is Only a Dream

I still think very many other things about the love of Jesus which are perhaps much stronger than what I am saying to you...What a joy to be humbled; it is the only thing that makes saints!... Can we doubt now the will of Jesus concerning our souls?... Life is only a *dream*, and soon we shall wake up, and what joy...the greater our sufferings are the more infinite will be our glory...Oh, let us not lose the trial that Jesus is sending us, it is a good mine to be exploited. Are we going to miss the chance?... The grain of sand wants to get to work, without *joy*, without *courage*, without *strength*, and it is all these titles which will facilitate the enterprise for it; it wants to work through love.

From a letter to her sister Céline | February 1889

THE PERFUME OF THE LILY

Each new suffering, each new agony of heart is like a light breeze which will carry to Jesus the perfume of His lily; then He will smile lovingly, and He will immediately prepare a new sorrow. He is filling the chalice to the brim, thinking that the more His lily grows in love the more, too, must it grow in suffering!... What a privilege Jesus grants us in sending such great *sorrow.* Ah! ETERNITY will not be too long to thank Him. He is giving us His favors just as He gave them to the greatest saints. Why this great predilection?...It is a secret which Jesus will reveal in our homeland on the day when "He will dry all the tears from our eyes."

From a letter to her sister Céline | MARCH 1889

LIVING THE VERY LIFE OF JESUS

Life is passing away...Eternity is advancing in great strides...
Soon we shall live the very life of Jesus...After having drunk at
the fountain of all sorrows, we shall be deified at the very fountain of all joys, all delights...Soon, little sister, with one look,
we shall be able to understand what is taking place within the
inner depths of our being...The image of this world is PASSING
AWAY...Soon we shall see new heavens, and a more radiant Sun
will light up with its splendors ethereal oceans and infinite horizons!...Immensity will be our domain...We shall no longer be
prisoners on this earth of exile...All will have PASSED AWAY...
Let us really offer our sufferings to Jesus to save souls, poor
souls!...They have less grace than we have, and still all the Blood
of God was shed to save them...And yet Jesus wills to make their
salvation depend on one sigh from our heart...What a mystery!
If one sigh can save *a soul*, what can sufferings like ours not
do?... Let us refuse Jesus nothing!

From a letter to her sister Céline | MARCH 1889

RESEMBLING JESUS

I admit that this word peace seemed a little strong to me, but the other day, when reflecting on it, I found the secret of suffering in peace...The one who says *peace* is not saying joy, or at least *felt* joy...To suffer in peace it is enough to will all that Jesus wills... To be the spouse of Jesus we *must* resemble Jesus, and Jesus is all bloody, He is crowned with thorns!

From a letter to her sister Céline | APRIL 1889

FALLING AT THE FEET OF JESUS

What does it matter, my Jesus, if I fall at each moment; I *see* my weakness through this and this is a great gain for me...*You can see* through this what I can do and now You will be more temped to carry me in Your arms...If You do not do it, it is because this pleases You to see me *on the ground*...Then I am not going to be disturbed, but I shall always stretch out my arms suppliant and filled with love!... I cannot believe the You would abandon me!

From a letter to her sister Céline | APRIL 1889

THE INEVITABLE SUFFERINGS OF LIFE

I would like nothing to be lacking to the perfect happiness of my dear little sister and that of my good cousin. But on earth there will always be some little cloud since life cannot go on without it, and since in heaven alone joy will be perfect. However, I desire that as much as possible God may spare those whom I love the inevitable sufferings of life, even if it means taking upon myself, if necessary, the trials He is reserving for them.

From a letter to Madame La Néele | OCTOBER 1891

JESUS ASKS LOVE FOR LOVE

Yes, I feel my desires are reborn. Perhaps after having asked us love for love, so to speak, Jesus will want to ask us blood for blood, life for life…In the meantime, we must let the bees draw out all the honey from the little calyxes, keeping nothing, giving all to Jesus, and then we shall say like the flower in the evening of our life: "The night, behold the night." Then it will be finished…And to the wintry blasts will succeed the gentle rays of the sun, to the tears of Jesus, eternal smiles…Ah, let us not refuse to weep with Him during one day since we shall enjoy His glory throughout all eternity.

From a letter to her sister Céline | OCTOBER 1891

THE AWAKENING OF JESUS

Jesus is there, *sleeping* as in days gone by, in the boat of the fishermen of Galilee. He is sleeping...and Céline does not *see* Him, for night has fallen on the boat...Céline *does not hear* the voice of Jesus. The wind is blowing...she *hears* it; she *sees* the darkness...and Jesus *is* always *sleeping*. However, if He were to awaken only for an instant, He would have only to command the wind and the sea, and there would be great calm. The night would become brighter than the day, Céline *would see the divine glance* of Jesus, and her soul would be consoled...But Jesus, too, would no longer be sleeping, and He is so FATIGUED!...His divine feet are tired from going after sinners, and Céline's boat Jesus is sleeping so peacefully...Oh, how happy Jesus is!

From a letter to her sister Céline | JULY 1893

GOD WANTS ONLY OUR WILL

But I felt something else, that frequently God wants only *our will*; He asks *all*, and if we were to refuse Him the least thing, He loves us too much to give in to us; however, as soon as our will is conformed to His, as soon as He sees we seek Him alone, then He conducts Himself with us as in the past He conducted Himself with Abraham...This is what Jesus is making me feel interiorly, and I think that you are on TRIAL, that *now* the cutting off is taking place which you feel is necessary...It is *now* that Jesus *is breaking* your *nature*, that He is giving you the cross and tribulation...Fear nothing. Here you will find more than anywhere else the cross and *martyrdom!*...We shall suffer together, as in the past Christians who used to join together in order to give each other more courage in the hour of trial...And then Jesus will come!

From a letter to her sister Céline | JULY 1894

THE BREVITY OF LIFE

This thought of the brevity of life gives me courage, it helps me bear with the weariness of the road. What does a little work on earth matter (says the Imitation)…we pass away and we have not here a lasting dwelling! Jesus has gone before us to prepare a place in the home of His Father, and then He will come and He will take us with Him so that where He is we also may be…Let us wait, let us suffer in peace, the hour of rest is approaching, the light of tribulations of this life of a moment are preparing us for an eternal weight of glory…

From a letter to Sr. Françoise Thérèse-Dosithee
(her sister Léonie) | JANUARY 1895

UNDERSTANDING THE VALUE OF SUFFERING

I have nothing to offer you, not even a *picture*, but I am mistaken, I will offer you tomorrow the divine *Reality*, Jesus-Victim, YOUR SPOUSE and mine…Dear little Sister, how sweet it is that we can, all five, call Jesus "Our Beloved." But what will it be when we shall see Him in heaven and follow Him everywhere, singing the same canticle only virgins are permitted to sing! Then we shall understand the value of suffering, and, like Jesus, we shall repeat: "It was really necessary that suffering should try us and have us come to glory."

From a letter to her sister Léonie | APRIL 1896

THE WOUNDS THAT JESUS RECEIVED

"I UNDERSTAND You, Jesus, but there is still a mystery I would like to fathom: Tell me, I beg You, why have You chosen the *dear sheep* of my shepherdess to try her?...If You had chosen strangers, the trial would have been sweeter..." Then showing the lamb His feet, His hands, and His heart, adorned with luminous wounds, the Good Shepherd answered: "Look at these wounds; they are the ones *I received in the house of those who loved Me*!...This is the reason why they are so beautiful, so glorious, and why for all eternity their brilliance will revive the joy of the angels and saints...Your shepherdess wonders what she has done to estrange her sheep, and *I*, what had I done to My people? In what had I made them sad?...Your dear Mother, then, must rejoice in having a share in My sorrows...If I am removing from her human support, it is only to fill her *very loving* heart!

From a letter to Mother Marie De Gonzague
(Prioress of Carmel) | JUNE 1896

LOVE AND SUFFERING AS WEAPONS

A Dieu, Brother...distance will never be able to separate our souls, death itself will make our union more intimate. If I go to heaven soon, I will ask Jesus' permission to go to visit you at Su-Tchuen, and we shall continue our apostolate together. In the meanwhile, I shall always be united to you by prayer, and I ask Our Lord never to allow me to rejoice when you are suffering. I would even wish that my brother always have consolation, and I trials; perhaps this is selfish?...But, no, since my only *weapon* is love and suffering and since your sword is that of the word and apostolic works.

From a letter to Père Adolphe Roulland
(member, Foreign Missions of Paris) | JULY 1896

THE GREATEST HONOR GOD CAN GIVE A SOUL

A Saint has said: "The greatest honor God can give a soul is not to give it much but to ask much from it! Jesus is treating you then as a privileged one. He wills that you already begin your mission and that through suffering you may save souls. Is it not in suffering, in dying that He Himself redeemed the world?...I know you aspire to the joy of sacrificing your life for the divine Master, but martyrdom of the heart is not less fruitful than the pouring out of one's blood, and now this martyrdom is yours. I am right, then, in saying that your lot is beautiful, that it is worthy of an apostle of Christ.

From a letter to Abbé Maurice Bellière
(member, Missionaries of Africa) | DECEMBER 1896

ACCOMPLISHING THE WILL OF JESUS IS JOY

Ah, if for a few moments you could read into my soul, how surprised you would be! The thought of heavenly bliss not only causes me not a single bit of joy, but I even ask myself at times how it will be possible to be happy without any suffering. Jesus no doubt will change my nature, otherwise I would miss suffering and the valley of tears. Never have I asked God to die young, this would have appeared to me as cowardliness; but He, from my childhood, saw fit to give me the intimate conviction that my course here below would be short. It is, then, the thought alone of accomplishing the Lord's will that makes up all my joy.

From a letter to Abbé Maurice Bellière
(member, Missionaries of Africa) | JULY 1897

Suffering without Sadness

Dear Mother, you know well that God has deigned to make me pass through many types of trials. I have suffered much since I was on earth, but, if in my childhood I suffered with sadness, it is no longer in this way that I suffer. It is with joy and peace. I am truly happy to suffer. O Mother, you must know all the secrets of my soul in order not to smile when you read these lines, for is there a soul less tried than my own if one judges by appearances? Ah! if the trial I am suffering for a year now appeared to the eyes of anyone, what astonishment would be felt!

Autobiography of a Soul | Chapter Ten

Jesus Can Do as He Pleases

For a long time I have not belonged to myself since I delivered myself totally to Jesus, and He is therefore free to do with me as He pleases. He has given me the attraction for a complete exile and He has made me *understand all the sufferings* I would meet with, asking me if I would want to drink this chalice to the dregs; I wanted to seize this cup immediately when Jesus presented it, but He withdrew His hand and made me understand that my resignation alone was pleasing to Him.

Autobiography of a Soul | Chapter Ten

FEARING NO EVIL IN THE SHADOW OF DEATH

Oh, my God, how gentle You are to the little victim of Your Merciful Love! Even now when You join exterior suffering to the trials of my soul, I cannot say: "The agonies of death have surrounded me," but I cry out in my gratitude: "I have descended into the valley of the shadow of death, nevertheless, I fear no evil because You are with me, Lord!"

From a letter to Sr. Geneviève of St. Teresa
(member of the Carmel in Lisieux) | AUGUST 1897

CHAPTER ELEVEN

The Little Way

"To be more than Carmelite,
Spouse and Mother."

Feeling More Than One Vocation

To be Your *Spouse*, to be a *Carmelite*, and by my union with You to be the *Mother* of souls, should not this suffice me? And yet it is not so. No doubt, these three privileges sum up my true *vocation: Carmelite, Spouse, Mother*, and yet I feel within me other *vocations*. I feel the *vocation* of the WARRIOR, THE PRIEST, THE APOSTLE, THE DOCTOR, THE MARTYR. Finally, I feel the need and the desire of carrying out the most heroic deeds for *You, O Jesus*. I feel within my soul the courage of the *Crusader*, the *Papal Guard*, and I would want to die on the field of battle in defense of the Church.

Autobiography of a Soul | CHAPTER NINE

HOW TO COMBINE THE CONTRASTS OF THE SOUL

I feel in me the *vocation* of the PRIEST. With what love, O Jesus, I would carry You in my hands when, at my voice, You would come down from heaven. And with what love would I give You to souls! But alas! While desiring to be a *Priest*, I admire and envy the humility of St. Francis of Assisi and I feel the *vocation* of imitating him in refusing the sublime dignity of the *Priesthood*. O Jesus, my Love, my Life, how can I combine these contrasts? How can I realize the desires of my poor *little soul*?...O my Jesus! What is your answer to all my follies? Is there a soul more *little*, more powerless than mine? Nevertheless even because of my weakness, it has pleased You, O Lord, to grant my *little childish desires* and You desire, today, to grant other desires that are *greater* than the universe.

Autobiography of a Soul | CHAPTER NINE

THE STILL MORE EXCELLENT WAY

Just as Mary Magdalene found what she was seeking by always stooping down and looking into the empty tomb, so I, abasing myself to the very depths of my nothingness, raised myself so high that I was able to attain my end. Without becoming discouraged, I continued my reading, and this sentence consoled me: "*Yet strive after THE BETTER GIFTS, and I point out to you a yet more excellent way.*" And the Apostle explains how all *the most PERFECT gifts* are nothing without *LOVE. That Charity is the EXCELLENT WAY that leads most surely to* God. I finally had rest.

Autobiography of a Soul | CHAPTER NINE

"My Vocation Is Love"

I understood that if the Church had a body composed of different members, the most necessary and most noble of all could not be lacking to it, and so I understood that the Church *had a Heart and this Heart was BURNING WITH LOVE. I understood that it was Love alone* that made the Church's members act, that if *Love* ever became extinct, apostles would not preach the Gospel and martyrs would not shed their blood. I understood that LOVE COMPRISED ALL VOCATIONS, THAT LOVE WAS EVERYTHING, THAT IT EMBRACED ALL TIMES AND PALCES...IN A WORD, THAT IT WAS ETERNAL!... Then in the excess of my delirious joy, I cried out: O Jesus, my Love...my *vocation*, at last I have found it...MY VOCATION IS LOVE!...I found my place in the Church and it is You, O my God, who have given me this place; in the heart of the Church, my Mother, I shall be *Love*. Thus I shall be everything, and thus my dream will be realized.

Autobiography of a Soul | Chapter Nine

BE BOLD IN WHAT WE ASK OF GOD

Behold, Lord, the counsel You give Your disciples after having told them that "The children of this world, in relation to their own generation, are more prudent than are the children of the light." A child of the light, I understood that *my desires of being everything*, of embracing all vocations, were the riches that would be able to render me unjust, so I made use of them *to make friends*. Remembering the prayer of Elisha to his Father Elijah when he dared to ask him for HIS DOUBLE SPIRIT, I presented myself before the angels and saints and I said to them: "I am the smallest of creatures; I know my misery and my feebleness, but I know also how much noble and generous hearts love to do good. I beg you then, O Blessed Inhabitants of heaven, I beg you to ADOPT ME AS YOUR CHILD. *To you alone will be the glory* which will make me merit, but deign to answer my prayer. It is bold, I know; however, I dare to ask you to obtain for me YOUR TWOFOLD LOVE.

Autobiography of a Soul | CHAPTER NINE

DOING THE SMALLEST THINGS THROUGH LOVE

Yes, my Beloved, this is how my life will be consumed. I have no other means of proving my love for you other than that of strewing flowers, that is, not allowing one little sacrifice to escape, not one look, one word, profiting by all the smallest things and doing them through love. I desire to suffer for love and even to rejoice through love; and in this way I shall strew flowers before You. While I am strewing my flowers, I shall sing, for could one cry while doing such a joyous action? I shall sing even when I must gather my flowers in the midst of thorns, and my song will be all the more melodious in proportion to the length and sharpness of the thorns.

Autobiography of a Soul | CHAPTER NINE

THE SMALLEST ACTS OF PURE LOVE

O my Jesus! I love You! I love the Church, my Mother! I recall that *"the smallest act of PURE LOVE is of more value to her than all other works together."* But is PURE LOVE in my heart? Are my measureless desires only but a dream, a folly? Ah! if this be so, Jesus, then enlighten me, for You know I am seeking only the truth. If my desires are rash, then make them disappear, for these desires are the greatest martyrdom to me. However, I feel, O Jesus, that after having aspired to the most lofty heights of Love, if one day I am not to attain them, I feel that I shall taste in the bosom of the *joy of the Fatherland,* unless You take away the memory of these earthly hopes through a miracle. Allow me, then, during my exile, the delights of love. Allow me to taste the sweet bitterness of my martyrdom.

Autobiography of a Soul | CHAPTER NINE

———❦———

JESUS'S WEAK LITTLE BIRD

O Jesus, Your *little bird* is happy to be *weak and little*. What would become of it if it were big? Never would it have the boldness to appear in Your presence, *to fall asleep* in front of you. Yes, this is still one of the weaknesses of the little bird; when it wants to fix its gaze upon the Divine Sun, and when the clouds prevent it from seeing a single ray of that Sun, in spite of itself, its little eyes close, its little head is hidden beneath its wing, and the poor little thing falls asleep believing all the time that it is fixing its gaze upon its Dear Star. When it awakens, it doesn't feel desolate; its little heart is at peace and it begins once again its work of *love*. It calls upon the angels and saints who rise like eagles before the consuming Fire, and since this is the object of the little bird's desire the eagles take pity on it, protecting and defending it, and putting to flight at the same time the vultures who want to devour it. These vultures are the demons whom the little bird doesn't fear, for it is not destined to be their *prey* but the prey of the *Eagle* whom it contemplates in the center of the Sun of Love.

Autobiography of a Soul | CHAPTER NINE

FLYING TOWARD THE SUN OF LOVE

Eternal Eagle, You desire to nourish me with Your divine substance and yet I am but a poor little thing who would return to nothingness if Your divine glance did not give me life from one moment to the next...Jesus, I am too little to perform great actions, and my own *folly* is this: to trust that Your Love will accept me as a victim. My *folly* consists in begging the eagles, my brothers, to obtain for me the favor of flying toward the Sun of Love with the *Divine Eagle's own wings*!

Autobiography of a Soul | CHAPTER NINE

THE SECRETS OF JESUS'S LOVE

O Jesus! Why can't I tell all *little* souls how unspeakable is Your condescension? I feel that if You found a soul weaker and littler than mine, which is impossible, You would be pleased to grant it still greater favors, provided it abandoned itself with total confidence to Your infinite Mercy. But why do I desire to communicate Your secrets of Love, O Jesus, for was it not You alone who taught them to me, and can You not reveal them to others? Yes, I know it, and I beg You to do it. I beg You to cast Your Divine Glance upon a great number of *little* souls. I beg You to choose a legion of Victims worthy of Your LOVE!

Autobiography of a Soul | CHAPTER NINE

BEING RAISED TO THE HEIGHTS OF SANCTITY

We are living now in an age of inventions, and we no longer have to take the trouble of climbing stairs, for, in the homes of the rich, an elevator has replaced these very successfully. I wanted to find an elevator which would raise me to Jesus for I am too small to climb the rough stairway of perfection. I searched then in the Scriptures for some sign of this elevator, the object of my desires, and I read these words coming from the mouth of Eternal Wisdom: "*Whoever is a LITTLE ONE, let him come to me.*" And so I succeeded. I felt I had found what I was looking for. But wanting to know, O my God, what You would do to *the very little one* who answered Your call, I continued my search and this is what I discovered: "*As one whom a mother caresses, so will I comfort you; you shall be carried at the breasts, and upon the knee they shall caress you.*" Ah! never did words more tender and more melodious come to give joy to my soul. The elevator which must raise me to heaven is Your arms, O Jesus! And for this I had no need to grow up, but rather I had to remain *little* and become this more and more.

Autobiography of a Soul | CHAPTER TEN

TO REMAIN ALWAYS POOR

Oh, dear Sister, I beg you, understand your little girl, understand that to love Jesus, to be His *victim of love*, the weaker one is, without desires or virtues, the more suited one is for the workings of this consuming and transforming Love…The *desire* alone to be a victim suffices, but we must consent to remain always poor and without strength, and this is the difficulty, for: "The truly poor in spirit, where do we find him? You must look for him from afar," said the Psalmist…He does not say that you must look for him among the great souls, but, "from afar," that is to say in *lowliness,* in *nothingness*…Ah! let us remain then *very far* from all that sparkles, let us love our littleness, let us love to feel nothing, then we shall be poor in spirit, and Jesus will come to look for us, and *however far* we may be, he will transform us in flames of love…

From a letter to Sr. Marie of the Sacred Heart
(her sister Marie) | SEPTEMBER 1896

DETACHED FROM THE WORRIES OF THE EARTH

It is a great trial to look on the *black* side, but this does not depend on you completely. Do what you *can*; detach your heart from the *worries* of this earth, and above all from creatures, and then be sure Jesus will do the *rest*. He will be unable to allow you to fall into the dreaded *mire*...Be consoled, dear little Sister, in heaven you will no longer *take a dark view of everything* but *a very bright* view...Yes, everything will be decked out in the divine *brightness* of our Spouse, the Lily of the valleys. *Together* we shall follow Him everywhere He goes...Ah! let us profit from the *short moment* of life...*together* let us please Jesus, let us save souls for Him by our sacrifices...Above all, let us be *little*, so that everybody may *trample* us underfoot, without our even having the appearance of feeling it and suffering from it.

From a letter to Sr. Marie of the Trinity
(one of St. Thérèse's novices) | JUNE 1897

ALWAYS RUN TOWARD JESUS

Ah! may Jesus pardon me if I have caused Him any pain, but He knows very well that while I do not have *the joy of faith*, I am trying to carry out its works at least. I believe I have made more acts of faith in this past year than all through my whole life. At each new occasion of combat, when my enemies provoke me, I conduct myself bravely. Knowing it is cowardly to enter into a duel, I turn my back on my adversaries without deigning to look them in the face; but I run toward my Jesus. I tell Him I am ready to shed my blood to the last drop to profess my faith in the existence of heaven. I tell Him, too, I am happy not to enjoy this beautiful heaven on this earth so that He will open it for all eternity to poor unbelievers.

Autobiography of a Soul | CHAPTER TEN

Chapter Twelve

The Way of Poverty

"He was rich and He made Himself poor."

GIVE YOUR WHOLE HEART TO JESUS

Marie of the Blessed Sacrament!...Your name speaks your mission...Console Jesus, make Him *loved* by souls...Jesus is sick, and we must state that the sickness of love is healed only through love!...Marie, really give your whole heart to Jesus, He is thirsty for it, He is hungry for it. Your heart, that is what He longs for, even to the point that to have it for Himself He consents to lodge under a dirty and hidden nook!... Ah! how not love a Friend who reduces Himself to such extreme indigence, and how does one dare speak of one's poverty when Jesus makes Himself like His fiancée...He was rich and HE made Himself poor in order to unite His poverty to the poverty of Marie of the Blessed Sacrament...What a mystery of love!

From a letter to her cousin Marie Guérin | July 1890

OUR NOTHINGNESS AND JESUS'S POWER

He despoils completely the souls dearest to Him. When seeing themselves is so great poverty, these poor little souls are fearful, it seems to them that they are good for nothing, since they receive all from others and can give nothing. But it is not so: the *essence* of their *being* is working in secret. *Jesus* forms in them the seed which must be developed up above in the celestial gardens of heaven. He is pleased to show them their nothingness and His power. He makes use of the *vilest* instruments so as to show them that He alone is working. He hastens to perfect His work for the day when the shadows having vanished, He will no longer use any intermediaries but an *eternal Face to Face!...*"

From a letter to her sister Céline | AUGUST 1893

POVERTY: THE BLIND HOPE IN GOD'S MERCY

My desires of martyrdom *are nothing*; they are not what give me the unlimited confidence that I feel in my heart. They are, to tell the truth, the spiritual riches that *render one unjust*, when one rests in them with complacence and when one believes they are *something great*...These desires are a *consolation* that Jesus grants at times to weak souls like mine (and these are numerous), but when He does not give this *consolation*, it is a great *privilege*. Recall the words of the Father: "The martyrs suffered with joy, and the King of Martyrs suffered with sadness." Yes, Jesus said, "Father, let this chalice pass away from me." Dear Sister, how can you say after this that my desires are the sign of my love?...Ah! I really feel that it is not this at all that pleases God in my little soul; what pleases Him is *that He sees me loving my littleness* and my *poverty, the blind hope that I have in His mercy*...that is my only treasure.

From a letter to Sr. Marie of the Sacred Heart
(her sister Marie) | SEPTEMBER 1896

GOD DOES NOT GIVE DESIRES HE CANNOT REALIZE

Oh, dear Sister, if you do not understand me, it is because you
are too great a soul...or rather it is because I am explaining
myself poorly, for I am sure that God would not give you the
desire to be POSSESSED by *Him*, by His *Merciful Love* if He
were not reserving this favor for you...or rather HE has already
given it to you, since you have given yourself to *Him*, since you
desire to be consumed by *Him*, and since God never gives desires
that He cannot realize.

From a letter to Sr. Marie of the Sacred Heart
(her sister Marie) | SEPTEMBER 1896

POVERTY OPENS US TO GOD'S GRACES

Since dear Aunt, I am only a *poor* grasshopper that has nothing
but its songs (again, it can sing only in the bottom of its heart,
not having a melodious voice), I will sing my most beautiful tune
on your feast day, and I will take care to have so touching a tone
that all the saints, taking pity on my poverty, will give me the
treasures of graces that I shall be delighted to offer to you.

From a letter to her aunt, Madame Guérin | NOVEMBER 1896

THE UNION OF SOULS FOR THE GOOD OF JESUS

It seems to me that the divine Savior has seen fit to unite our souls in working for the salvation of sinners, just as HE united in the past, the souls of the Venerable Père de la Colombiere and Blessed Margaret Mary. I was reading recently in the *Life* of this saint: "One day, when I was approaching Our Lord to receive Him in Holy Communion, He showed His Sacred Heart as a burning furnace and the other hearts (her own and that of P. de la Colombiere) that were about to be united and engulfed in It, saying: 'It is thus that My pure love unites three hearts forever.' He made me understand that this union was for His glory, and for this reason He willed us to be like brother and sister, equally endowed with spiritual goods. Then I pointed out to Our Lord my poverty and the inequality there was between a priest of such great virtue and a poor sinner like me, and He said, 'The infinite riches of My Heart will make up for everything and will equalize everything.'"…Jesus has chosen me to be the sister of one of His apostles, and the words that the "holy Lover of His Heart' addressed to Him out of *humility*, I repeat to Him *myself* in *all truth*; so I hope that His infinite riches will make up for all that I lack in accomplishing the work He entrusts to me.

From a letter to Abbé Maurice Bellière
(member, Missionaries of Africa) | April 1897

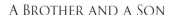

A BROTHER AND A SON

If, as I believe, my father and mother are in heaven, they must be looking at and blessing the brother whom Jesus has given me. They had so much wanted a missionary son!...I have been told that before my birth my parents were hoping their prayer was finally going to be realized. Had they been able to pierce the veil of the future, they would have seen it was indeed through me their desire was fulfilled; since a missionary has become my brother, he is also their son, and in their prayers they cannot separate the brother from his unworthy sister.

From a letter to Père Adolphe Roulland
(member, Foreign Missionaries of Paris) | May 1897

FOR THE GLORY OF GOD

I hope, *Monsieur l'abbé*, that you will continue to pray for me who am not an angel as you appear to believe, but a poor little Carmelite, who is very imperfect and who in spite of her poverty has, like you, the desire to work for the glory of God.

From a letter to Abbé Maurice Bellière
(member, Missionaries of Africa) | December 1896

DEATH IS A CELEBRATION

I beg you, dear little Brother, try like her to convince yourself that instead of losing me you *will find* me, and that I will no longer leave you. Ask the same favor for the Mother whom you love and whom I love still more than you love her, since she is my visible Jesus. I would give you with joy what you are asking if I had not made the vow of poverty, but because of it I cannot even dispose of a picture. Our Mother alone can satisfy you, and I know she will grant your desires. Precisely in view of my approaching death, a Sister took my photograph for our Mother's feast day. The novices cried out when seeing me that I had taken on my grand look; it seems that usually I am smiling more, but believe, little Brother, that if my photograph is not smiling at you, my *soul* will not cease *to smile at you* when it is near you. *A Dieu, dear and much loved Brother*; believe that I shall be for all eternity your *true little* sister Thérèse of the Child Jesus.

From a letter to Abbé Maurice Bellière
(member, Missionaries of Africa) | JULY 1897

It Is Poverty That Attracts Jesus

Perhaps you remember how in the past I used to love calling myself "Jesus' little plaything." Even now I am happy to be this; however, I have thought that the divine Child had many other souls filled with sublime virtues who call themselves "His toys." I thought, then, they were His *beautiful toys* and my poor soul was only a *little* toy without any value...to console myself, I said: Often little children are more pleased with *little toys* that they can *leave* aside or *take up, break* or *kiss* at their whim than with others of a greater value which they almost dare not touch...Then I rejoiced at being *poor*, I wanted to become this more and more each day, in order that Jesus may take more delight *in playing* with me.

From a letter to Sister Françoise Thérèse-Dosithee, VHM
(her sister Léonie) | APRIL 1895

POVERTY OF SPIRIT: PRACTICING WHAT ONE TEACHES

Mother, I would not be able to explain these sad sentiments of
nature if I had not felt them in my own heart, and I would like
to entertain the sweet illusion that they visited only my heart,
but you commanded me to listen to the temptations of your dear
little novices. I learned very much when carrying out the mission
you entrusted to me; above all I was forced to practice what I
was teaching others. And so now I can say that Jesus has given
me the grace of not being any more attached to the goods of the
mind and heart than to those of earth. If it happens that I think
or say something that is pleasing to my Sisters, I find it very
natural that they take it as a good that belongs to them.

Autobiography of a Soul | CHAPTER ELEVEN

POVERTY PRESERVES THE HEART

At the age of ten the heart allows itself to be easily dazzled, and I consider it a great grace not to have remained at Alencon. The friends we had there were too worldly; they knew too well how to ally the joys of this earth to the service of God. They didn't think about *death* enough, and yet *death* had paid its visit to a great number of those whom I knew, the young, the rich, the happy! I love to return in spirit to the *enchanting* places where they lived, wondering where these people are, what became of their houses and gardens where I saw them enjoy life's luxuries? And I see that all is vanity and vexation of spirit under the sun, that the *only good* is to love God with all one's heart and to be *poor in spirit* here on earth.

Autobiography of a Soul | CHAPTER FOUR

FINDING ONE'S JOY IN POVERTY OF SPIRIT

(At the beginning of my spiritual life when I was thirteen or fourteen, I used to ask myself what I would have to strive for later on because I believed it was quite impossible for me to understand perfection better. I learned very quickly since then that the more one advances, the more one sees the goal is still far off. And now I am simply resigned to see myself always imperfect and in this I find my joy.)

Autobiography of a Soul | CHAPTER SEVEN

"NOTHING IS MINE"

I was saying: Jesus does not want me to lay claim to what belongs to me; and this should seem easy and natural to me since *nothing is mine*. I have renounced the goods of this earth through the Vow of Poverty, and so I haven't the right to complain when one takes a thing that is not mine. On the contrary, I should rejoice when it happens that I feel the pinch of poverty.

Autobiography of a Soul | Chapter Ten

THE INCOMPARABLE JOY OF SPIRITUAL POVERTY

Ah! what peace floods the soul when she rises above the natural feelings. No, there is no joy comparable to that which the truly poor in spirit experience. If such a one asks for something with detachment, and if this thing is not only refused but one tries to take away what one already has, the poor in spirit follow Jesus's counsel: "*If anyone take away your coat, let go your cloak as well.*"

Autobiography of a Soul | Chapter Ten

CHAPTER THIRTEEN

The Way of Eucharist

"How is it possible that God can be present in a small host?"

THE WAY OF SIMPLE LOVE

SPIRITUAL CONFERENCES ON HOLY COMMUNION

We carried on *spiritual conferences* together frequently. Here is a sample taken form one of Mama's letters: "Our two little dears, Céline and Thérèse, are angels of benediction, little cherubs. Thérèse is the joy and happiness of Marie and even her glory; it's incredible how proud she is of her. It's true she has very rare answers for one her age; she surpasses Céline in this who is twice her age. Céline said the other day: 'How is it that God can be present in a small host?' The little one said: 'That is not surprising, God is all powerful.' 'What does all powerful mean?' "It means He can do what He wants.'

Autobiography of a Soul | CHAPTER ONE

VISITS TO THE BLESSED SACRAMENT

Each afternoon I took a walk with Papa. We made our visit to the Blessed Sacrament together, going to a different church each day, and it was in this way we entered the Carmelite chapel for the first time. Papa showed me the choir grille and told me there were nuns behind it. I was far from thinking at that time that nine years later I would be in their midst!

Autobiography of a Soul | CHAPTER TWO

THE CELEBRATION OF FEAST DAYS

The *feasts!* What memories this word brings back to me. How I love the *feasts!* You knew how to explain all the mysteries hidden under each and you did it so well that they were truly heavenly days for me. I loved above all the processions in honor of the Blessed Sacrament. What a joy it was for me to throw flowers beneath the feet of God! Before allowing them to fall to the ground, I threw them as high as I could and I was never so happy as when I saw my roses *touch* the sacred monstrance.

Autobiography of a Soul | CHAPTER FOUR

HEAVEN ITSELF IN OUR SOUL

Oh! no, the absence of Mama didn't cause me any sorrow on the day of my First Communion. Wasn't Heaven itself in my soul, and hadn't Mamma taken her place there a long time ago? Thus in receiving Jesus' visit, I received also Mama's. She blessed me and rejoiced at my happiness. I was not crying because of Pauline's absence. I would have been happy to see her by my side, but for a long time I had accepted my sacrifice of her. On that day, joy alone filled my heart and I united myself to her who gave herself irrevocably to Him who gave Himself so lovingly to me!

Autobiography of a Soul | CHAPTER FOUR

RECEIVING JESUS REGULARLY

The day after my First Communion was still beautiful, but it was tinged with a certain melancholy. The beautiful dress Marie had bought me, all the gifts I had received did not satisfy my heart. Only Jesus could do this, and I longed for the moment when I could receive Him a second time. About a month after my First Communion, I went to confession for the Ascension and I dared ask permission to receive Holy Communion. Against all hope, the priest permitted it and so I had the happiness of kneeling at the communion railing between Papa and Marie. What a sweet memory I have of this second visit of Jesus! My tears flowed again with an ineffable sweetness, and I repeated to myself these words of St. Paul: "It is no longer I that live, it is Jesus who lives in me!"

Autobiography of a Soul | CHAPTER FOUR

COMMUNION THANKSGIVINGS

Often during my Communions, I repeated these words of the *Imitation*: "O Jesus, unspeakable *sweetness*, change all the consolations of this earth into *bitterness* for me." This prayer fell from my lips without constraints; it seemed I repeated it not with my will but like a child who repeats the words a person he loves has inspired in him.

Autobiography of a Soul | CHAPTER FOUR

THE TERRIBLE SPIRITUAL SICKNESS OF SCRUPLES

The year following my First Communion passed almost entirely without any interior trials for my soul. It was during my retreat for the second Communion that I was assailed by the terrible sickness of scruples. One would have to pass through this martyrdom to understand it well, and for me to express what I suffered for *a year and a half* would be impossible. All my most simple thoughts and actions became the cause of trouble for me, and I had relief only when I told them to Marie. This cost me dearly, for I believed I was obliged to tell her the absurd thoughts I had even about her. As soon as I laid down my burden, I experienced peace for an instant; but this peace passed away like a lightning flash, and soon my martyrdom began over again.

Autobiography of a Soul | CHAPTER FOUR

JESUS OUR TRUE FRIEND

No one paid attention to me, and I would go up to the choir of the chapel and remain before the Blessed Sacrament until the moment when Papa came to get me. This was my only consolation, for was not Jesus my *only Friend*? I knew how to speak only to Him; conversations with creatures, even pious conversations, fatigued my soul. I felt it was far more valuable to speak to God than to speak about Him, for there is so much self-loving intermingled with spiritual conversations.

Autobiography of a Soul | CHAPTER FOUR

THE SOUL IS THE LIVING TEMPLE OF THE HOLY TRINITY

For a grace received faithfully, He granted a multitude of others. He gave Himself to me in Holy Communion more frequently than I would have dared hope. I'd taken as a rule of conduct to receive, without missing a single one, the Communions my confessor permitted, allowing him to regulate the number and not asking. At this time in my life, I didn't have the *boldness* I now have, for I'm very sure a soul must tell her confessor the attraction she feels to receive God. It is not to remain in a golden ciborium that He comes to us *each day* from heaven; it's to find another heaven, infinitely more dear to Him than the first; the heaven of our soul, made to His image, the living temple of the adorable Trinity!

Autobiography of a Soul | CHAPTER FIVE

To Receive Jesus in His House

Our greatest consolation was to receive *Jesus Himself* in His *house* and to be His living temple in the very place He had honored with His presence. As is the custom in Italy, the Blessed Sacrament is reserved on only one altar in the churches, and here alone can one receive Holy Communion. This altar was in the Basilica itself where the Holy House is to be found, enclosed like a precious diamond in a white marble casket. This didn't satisfy Céline and me! It was in the *diamond* not in the *casket* that we wanted to receive Holy Communion. Papa with his customary gentleness did like all the rest, but Céline and I went in search of a priest who had accompanied us everywhere and who was just then preparing to say Mass in the Santa Casa by special privilege. He asked for *two small hosts* which he laid alongside the large one on the paten and you can well understand, dear Mother, the joy we *both* experienced at receiving Communion in the blessed house!

Autobiography of a Soul | Chapter Six

BEING RECEIVED INTO CARMEL

On the morning of the great day, casting a last look upon Les Buissonets, that beautiful cradle of my childhood which I was never to see again, I left on my dear King's arm to climb Mount Carmel. As on the evening before, the whole family was reunited to hear Holy Mass and receive Communion. As soon as Jesus descended into the hearts of my relatives, I heard nothing around me but sobs. I was the only one who didn't shed any tears, but my heart was beating *so violently* it seemed impossible to walk when they signaled for me to come to the enclosure door. I advanced, however, asking myself whether I was going to die because of the beating of my heart! Ah! what a moment that was! One would have to experience it to know what it is.

Autobiography of a Soul | CHAPTER SEVEN

THE REPOSE OF JESUS IN OUR SOULS

It seems to me that when Jesus descends into my heart He is content to find Himself so well received and I, too, am content. All this, however, does not prevent both distractions and sleepiness from visiting me, but at the end of the thanksgiving when I see that I've made it so badly, I make a resolution to be thankful all through the rest of the day. You see dear Mother, that I am far from being on the way off fear; I always find a way to be happy and to profit from my miseries; no doubt this does not displease Jesus since He seems to encourage me on this road.

Autobiography of a Soul | CHAPTER EIGHT

JESUS HIDDEN IN THE EUCHARIST

O Divine Word! You are the Adored Eagle whom I love and who alone *attracts me*! Coming into this land of exile, You willed to suffer and to die in order *to draw* souls to the bosom of the Eternal Fire of the Blessed Trinity. Ascending once again to the Inaccessible Light, henceforth Your abode, You remain still in this "valley of tears," hidden beneath the appearances of a white host. Eternal Eagle, You desire to nourish me with Your divine substance and yet I am but a poor little thing who would return to nothingness if Your divine glance did not give me life from one moment to the next.

Autobiography of a Soul | CHAPTER NINE

The Eucharist Is the Command to Love

[At] the Last Supper, when He knew the heats of His disciples were burning with a more ardent love for Him who had just given Himself to them in the unspeakable mystery of His Eucharist, this sweet Savior wished to give them a *new commandment*. He said to them with inexpressible tenderness: "*A new commandment I give you that you love one another*" *THAT AS I HAVE LOVED YOU, YOU ALSO LOVE ONE ANOTHER. By this will all men know that you are my disciples,* if you have love for one another."

Autobiography of a Soul | CHAPTER TEN

GAINING PRIESTLY BROTHERS

It was our Holy Mother St. Teresa who sent me my first little brother…I was in the laundry, very much occupied by my work, when Mother Agnes of Jesus took me aside and read a letter she had just received. It was from a young seminarian, inspired by St. Teresa of Avila. He was asking for a Sister who would devote herself especially to the salvation of his soul and aid him through her prayers and sacrifices when he was a missionary so that he could save many souls. He promised to remember the one who would become his sister at the Holy Sacrifice each day after he was ordained. Mother Agnes of Jesus told me she wanted me to become the sister of this future missionary…Mother, it would be impossible for me to express my happiness. My desire, answered in this unexpected way, gave birth in my heart to a joy which I can describe only as that of a child.

Autobiography of a Soul | CHAPTER ELEVEN

THE ABSENCE OF CONSOLATIONS IN HOLY COMMUNION

Don't be troubled about feeling no consolation in your Communions; this is a trial that you must bear with love. Don't lose any of the *thorns* you are meeting every day; with one of them you can *save a soul*!... Ah, if you only knew how much God is offended! Your soul is so well made for consoling Him... love Him to *folly* for all those who don't love Him!

From a letter to her cousin Marie Guérin | JULY 1889

ACCEPTING THAT WHICH JESUS LONGS TO GIVE US

This morning, during my Holy Communion, I prayed very much to Jesus to give you His joys; alas! This is not what He is sending us for some time. It is the Cross, the Cross alone, which He is giving us in order to test us...Oh! Aunt, if it had been only myself who was suffering, this would been nothing, but I know the large share you took in our trial. For your feast, I would love to take away all sorrow and to take for myself all your pains. This is what I was asking just now from Him whose Heart beats in unison with my own. I then felt that all He could give us of the best was suffering, and He was giving this only to His *chosen* friends; this answer proved to me that I was not answered, for I saw that Jesus loved dear Aunt to take away the Cross!

From a letter to her aunt, Madame Guérin | NOVEMBER 1888

Choosing Freely the Way to Follow Jesus

Perhaps Jesus wanted to show me the world before His *first visit* to me in order that I may choose freely the way I was to follow. The time of my First Communion remains engraved in my heart as a memory without any clouds. It seems to me I could not have been better disposed to receive Him than I was, and all my spiritual trials had left me for nearly a whole year. Jesus wished to make me taste a joy as perfect as is possible in this vale of tears.

Autobiography of a Soul | Chapter Four

Communion Is Not for Us Alone

I am thinking, too, of my little sister Marie. It seems to be that since she has placed her abode in the *treetops*, I must appear to her very little and insignificant. When approaching the heavens, we discover marvels that are not met in the humble valley. She will say I am naughty, but this will not stop me from receiving Holy Communion for her *Highness* on hear feast day.

From a letter to her aunt, Madame Guérin | August 1893

RECEIVING COMMUNION OFTEN

Dear little sister, *receive Communion often*, very often...That is the *only remedy* if you want to be healed, and Jesus hasn't placed this attraction in your soul for nothing. (I believe that He would be pleased if you could receive the two Communions you missed, for, then the devil's victory would be less great since he would not have succeeded in separating Jesus from your heart.)

From a letter to her cousin, Marie Guérin | JANUARY 1889

LOVE IN THE HEARTS OF MOTHERS

Dear little Aunt, when repeating (how much I love you), I have no fear of boring you, and this is the reason making me think this way. When I am before the Tabernacle, I can say only one thing to Our Lord: "My God, you know that I love You." And I feel my prayer does not tire Jesus; knowing the helplessness of His poor little spouse, He is content with her good will. I know, too, that God has poured something of the love overflowing His Heart into the hearts of mothers...And the one to whom I am speaking has received such a large measure of maternal love that I cannot have any fear of being misunderstood.

From a letter to her aunt, Madame Guérin | November 1893

OFFERING COMMUNION FOR OTHERS

Our two good Mothers and all your little sisters send you and Francis their love. I am not forgetting that tomorrow we celebrate the feast of St. Luke, one of His patrons, so I will offer my Holy Communion for him, and I will ask Jesus to reward him for the trouble he is taking to find remedies for me.

From a letter to Madame La Néele | OCTOBER 1895

COMMUNION AS THANKSGIVING

I notice in my letter that never shall I have the space to say all I would like. I would like, dear Relatives, to speak to you in detail of my Holy Communion this morning which you made so touching or rather so triumphant by your bundles of flowers. I am allowing dear little Marie of the Eucharist to tell you all the details, and I want only to tell you that she sang, before Communion, a little couplet that I had composed for this morning. When Jesus was in my heart, she sang this couplet from *Vivre d'Amour*: "To die by love is a very sweet martyrdom." I cannot express to you how high and beautiful her voice was; she had promised me not to cry in order to please me, and my hopes were surpassed. Good Jesus must have *heard* and understood perfectly what I expect from Him, and it was exactly what I wanted!

From a letter to Monsieur and Madame Guérin | JULY 1897

Two Prayers of Saint Thérèse

A Letter Saint Thérèse Carried on Her Heart on the Day of Her Profession, September 8, 1890

O Jesus, my Divine Spouse! May I never lose the second robe of my baptism! Take me before I can commit the slightest voluntary fault. May I never seek nor find anything but Yourself alone. May creatures be nothing for me and may I be nothing for them, but may You, Jesus, be *everything*! May the things of earth never be able to trouble my soul, and may nothing disturb my peace. Jesus, I ask You for nothing but peace, and also love, infinite love without any limits other than Yourself; love which is no longer I but You, my Jesus. Jesus, may I die a martyr for You. Give me martyrdom of heart or of body, or rather give me both. Give me the grace to fulfill my Vows in all their perfection, and make me understand what a real spouse of Yours should be. Never let me be a burden to the community, let nobody be occupied with me, let me be looked upon as one to be trampled underfoot, forgotten like Your little grain of sand, Jesus. May Your will be done in me perfectly, and may I arrive at the place You have prepared for me.

Jesus, allow me to save very many souls; let no soul be lost today; let all the souls in purgatory be saved. Jesus, pardon me if I say anything I should not say. I want only to give You joy and to console You.

Act of Oblation to Merciful Love

J. M. J. T.

Offering of myself as a Victim of Holocaust to God's Merciful Love

O My God! Most Blessed Trinity, I desire to *Love* You and make You *Loved*, to work for the glory of Holy Church by saving souls on earth and liberating those suffering in purgatory. I desire to accomplish Your will perfectly and to reach the degree of glory You have prepared for me in Your Kingdom. I desire, in a word, to be a saint, but I feel my helplessness and beg You, O my God! To be Yourself my *Sanctity*!

Since You loved me so much as to give me Your only Son as my Savior and my Spouse, the infinite treasures of His merits are mine. I offer them to You with gladness, begging You to look upon me only in the Face of Jesus and in His heart beating with *Love*.

I offer You, too, all the merits of the saints (in heaven and on earth), their acts of *Love*, and those of the holy angels. Finally, I offer You, *O Blessed Trinity!* The *Love* and merits of the *Blessed Virgin, my dear Mother*. It is to her I abandon my offering, begging her to present it to You. Her Divine Son, my *Beloved* Spouse, told us in the days of His mortal life: "*Whatsoever you ask the Father in my name he will give it to you!*" I am certain, then, that You will grant my desires; I know O my God! that *the more You want to give, the more You make us desire*. I feel in my heart immense desires and it is with confidence I ask You to come and take possession of my soul. Ah! I cannot receive Holy Communion as often as I desire, but, Lord are You not *all-powerful?* Remain in men as in a tabernacle and never separate Yourself from Your little victim.

I want to console You for the ingratitude of the wicked, and I beg of You to take away my freedom to displease You. If through weakness I sometimes fall, may Your *Divine Glance* cleanse my soul immediately, consuming all my imperfections like the fire that transforms everything into itself.

I thank You, O my God! For all the graces You have granted me, especially the grace of making me pass through the crucible of suffering. It is with joy I shall contemplate You on the Last Day carrying the scepter of Your Cross. Since You deigned to give me a share in this very precious Cross, I hope in heaven to resemble You and to see shinning in my glorified body the sacred stigmata of Your Passion.

After earth's Exile, I hope to go and enjoy You in the Fatherland, but I do not want to lay up merits for heaven. I want to work for Your *Love alone* with the one purpose of pleasing You, consoling Your Sacred Heart, and saving souls who will love You eternally.

In the evening of this life, I shall appear before You with empty hands, for I do not ask You, Lord, to count my works. All our justice is stained in Your eyes. I wish, then, to be clothed in Your own *Justice* and to receive from Your *Love* the eternal possession of *Yourself!* I want no other *Throne*, no other *Crown* but You, my *Beloved!*

Time is nothing in Your eyes, and a single day is like a thousand years. You can, then, in one instant prepare me to appear before You.

In order to live in one single act of perfect Love, I OFFER MYSELF AS A VICTIM OF HOLOCAUST TO YOUR MERCIFUL LOVE, asking You to consume me incessantly, allowing the waves of *infinite tenderness* shut up within You to overflow into my soul, and that thus I may become a *martyr* of Your *Love, O my God!*

May this martyrdom, after, having prepared me to appear before You, finally cause me to die and may my soul take its flight without any delay into the eternal embrace of *Your Merciful Love.*

I want, O my *Beloved*, at each beat of my heart to renew this offering to You an infinite number of times, until the shadows having disappeared I may be able to tell You of my *Love* in an *Eternal Face to Face!*

Marie-Françoise-Thérèse of the Child Jesus and the Holy Face, unworthy Carmelite religious.

This 9th day of June

Feast of the Most Holy Trinity

In the year of grace, 1895